MAR     2009

# The Ties That Bind

# Also by Bertice Berry

*A Memoir of Race,*

# The Ties That Bind

*Memory, and Redemption*

# BERTICE BERRY

BROADWAY BOOKS
NEW YORK

BROADWAY

Published in the United States by Broadway Books,
an imprint of The Doubleday Publishing Group,
a division of Random House, Inc., New York.
www.broadwaybooks.com

BROADWAY BOOKS and its logo, a letter B bisected on
the diagonal, are trademarks of Random House, Inc.

*Book design by Jennifer Ann Daddio*

Library of Congress Cataloging-in-Publication Data
Berry, Bertice.
The ties that bind: a memoir of race, memory, and
redemption / by Bertice Berry. — 1st ed.
p.    cm.
1. Berry, Bertice—Family. 2. African Americans—Biography.
3. African American families. 4. Freeman, John Henry, d.
1929 or 30. 5. Hunn, John, 1818–1894. 6. Underground
Railroad—Delaware. 7. Berry, Bertice—Childhood and youth.
8. Wilmington (Del.)—Biography. 9. Slavery—Social
aspects—United States—History. 10. United States—Race
relations. I. Title.

E185.96.B46 2009
973.7'115—dc22
2008025555

ISBN 978-0-7679-2414-6

PRINTED IN THE UNITED STATES OF AMERICA

1 3 5 7 9 10 8 6 4 2

First Edition

For

Beatrice Berry,

John Henry Freeman, Annie Mae Freeman,

Caroline Freeman,

and

John Hunn

# CONTENTS

*Part Two*

# Race

*Part Three*

# Redemption

# *Where I'm Coming From*

If you ask any Afro-wearing, Nikki Giovanni–loving black woman born in the sixties what her greatest fear is, she will tell you that right up there with the fear of her child being pulled over by the policeman who missed his one day of diversity training is the fear of being called an "Oreo," or, worse yet, a honky lover.

I grew up with proud role models like Angela Davis, Malcolm X, and Jesus. Somewhere in the mental state of what I call "Negrophrenia" (a term I coined to describe blacks who distrust whites, but aspire to be like them), I came to believe that all blacks were descendants of African royalty, and that all whites were directly or indirectly responsible for slavery and its repercussions on African American society. When I was younger, I had no time for howdy-do Negroes who shuffled along saying things like, "Some of my best friends are white."

I was a soul sista through and through. I worked hard to make sure that no one called me an Oreo (black on the outside, white on the inside). And yet that's exactly what happened when I graduated from my all-black, separate and unequal high school in Wilmington, Delaware, and matriculated at the lily-white campus at Jacksonville University in Florida.

My college choices had been narrowed down to JU and a historically black university, Norfolk State, where I had planned to go with my childhood friend Tia and another class-mate. While Tia and her parents told me that I should go to Florida, my other friend called me the names I feared most. According to him, I had turned my back on my people in favor of the white man's school. But Tia consoled me and said that I would be a fool to pass up the opportunity to see the world from the other side.

"You better do the right thing, hussy," Tia said, using her term of endearment. "This is a once-in-a-lifetime chance," she said. Tia knew that I had been "found" by a wealthy bene-factor who wanted to help educate a deserving poor black stu-dent. I wasn't sure about the deserving part, but I was certainly black and poor. While Tia and her family were coaxing me to do what I considered at the time to be the "white" thing, my other friend told me that I was a sellout, an Oreo.

Many African Americans face the fear of being thought of as "not black enough." It is this fear that sometimes moves us away from our more holistic self, a self that is connected to a world that goes beyond black and white. This fear of not being black enough kept me from looking at a much larger story, a story that was all too obvious and easy to find.

When I was growing up in Wilmington, Delaware, my mother frequently told me about her grandfather, John Henry Freeman, the man who raised her. When she was still a child, John Henry would tell her stories of his life in the mid-1800s. To her, his stories were of happy times and noble whites, something that made little sense to me as a child, and even less as I got older.

When my mother told me my great-grandfather's stories, I refused to believe them on the grounds that they simply were not black enough. The main character in my great-grandfather's stories was white, and he was good. My beliefs about life in the 1800s did not allow this to be true, so rather than research and look for evidence, I rejected the stories completely. But life is a highway full of twists and turns. If you follow the road willingly, you'll find that the path connects itself back around to the point of origin.

Few people ever find this place; most don't even know to look.

# The Ties That Bind

# INTRODUCTION

My journey from the bondage of the past to freedom started with *Redemption Song*, a novel I wrote in 2000:

> *My children, my children of Grace, you're gonna have to start the family over. It's on to you to set things straight.*
>
> *Y'all done traded one slavery from another when you turned your back on wisdom. You ain't free to do what you want to do; you free to do what you supposed to do. Find out what you're here for, what you were sent for.*

*Take care of children. Just 'cause they don't come from you don't mean they don't belong to you. Come back to truth. Tell others that they can't hate their masters and want to be like him. Tell them all they did when they were slaves. How they worked together and take care of one another. Tell them all they do with nothing, and how they make everything work for somebody else. They can learn they history. Tell them to love, to forgive, to never forget.*

*They have to stand ground 'cause bigger change than they seen is coming. You the beginning of that change, but be careful. Change never comes without struggle . . . and joy never comes without pain.*

*In your lifetime you will see a big struggle, but you have each other to get through it.*

*Don't let the little things keep you from doing the big things. Others will try to stop you, but things are already moving; they can't be stopped. Everybody who looks like you is not on your side. And everybody who don't, ain't against you.*

*Talk to God and never stop loving. The more I write the more I see, the more I see the more I know everything is gonna be okay. I can feel it. I'm leaving these papers right here 'cause I know they gonna find you.*

*It's my time and I feel that, too. Learn from the past that's yours. Take the gift of what I done seen and use it to love. This is the Recipe of Life; the road to freedom. Freedom ain't just about living free it's about being free. The chains on our wrists ain't as strong as the chains on our mind. The only thing that*

*can win over that evil is love. So learn to love, strive to love,*
*'cause we ain't got time for nothing else.*

Those words were, and still are, a comforting gift. I had no idea how prophetic they would come to be.

*Redemption Song* is a story about love and the connections of African Americans to their historical past. It opens in modern times with a couple, Ross and Fina, who happen upon the same bookstore on the same day. They are both looking for the only copy of a slave narrative called *Children of Grace*. The book was written by a woman named Iona, who during slavery lived in deplorable conditions. In the midst of her pain, Iona found love. But her love, a man named Joe, was sold away from her. Iona was savagely raped by the slave owner and had a child, who was also sold away. Joe eventually gets to freedom and fathers a child. Still, he longs for his Iona. Joe ventures back into slavery to purchase Iona's freedom, which he does, but then is killed the next morning.

Iona's pain is so deep that she can barely carry on, but she perseveres, for she knows that her future depends on it. Through a moving of the Spirit, Iona begins to write the story of her life so that someday her descendants and Joe's will find one another and complete the cycle of love that they started years before.

Generations later, when Ross and Fina (who are descendants of Joe and Iona) find Iona's book, and eventually fall in love, Iona's desire is fulfilled and her joy is made complete.

When the book was published, I was certain that I had done my ancestors proud. To a great degree I had, but a half-truth is not the truth; it is an incomplete version of the whole picture.

When it comes to righting the wrongs of history, everyone, both black and white, must play a part. If we are to move beyond the sins of slavery we must honor our ancestors. We must tell their stories, we must confess, we must forgive, and we must give thanks. We must take a closer look at our personal history and the history of this country. When we do, a fuller story will emerge, a story that is neither all black nor all white, all good nor all evil. This story exists on a continuum of truth; once observed fully and honestly it has the ability to set us free.

The question then is, what is freedom? Even now, when one of my children asks, "Mommy, when did black people become free?" I am forced to first take a deep breath, find a comfortable chair, and say, "Well, that's not an easy answer."

Slavery was officially abolished in America in 1865, a full two years after Lincoln signed the Emancipation Proclamation. It was not until 1866, when slave codes were nullified, that blacks were considered U.S. citizens. Then, in 1866, the Fourteenth Amendment was signed, granting blacks equal rights and equal citizenship. Black men got the right to vote in 1870, when, under the Fifteenth Amendment, suffrage was granted to all male citizens. In 1875, Congress passed the Civil Rights Act, which granted equal treatment for blacks in public, but overturned it in 1883. It was not until 1957 that a new Civil Rights Act was passed, and six years after that, in 1963, Dr. Martin Luther King Jr. declared, "One hundred years later [after a great American signed the Emancipation Proclamation] the Negro still is not free."

African Americans have had a tremendous journey from slavery to the present; but true freedom is not just physical, it is emotional and spiritual as well. It's obvious that the tremendous task of ending slavery in this country was only the beginning of freedom for blacks in general. This requires that we become free of the negative impact that slavery has on all Americans, black and white. It requires that we look closely at how we perceive ourselves and how others perceive us, and demands that we have a better understanding of our past history and that of our ancestors, both black and white.

My own journey to liberty has been fraught with twists and turns, with complexity and irony. I have had to both forgive and repent.

When I wrote *Redemption Song*, I wrote a fictionalized version of some of the things that actually happened during slavery. I incorporated real accounts of the horrors that took place within that "peculiar institution." I wanted people to know and never forget. My intentions were good, but I was off base and didn't know it at the time.

In my attempt to tell a story of love that took place during slavery, I made one of my greatest errors. When I named the evil slave owner, I gave him the name of the man who owned the plantation that my family had lived on during that period. It made so much sense to me then. By using his name, I was putting him on record, calling him on the carpet. I put him right up there on what could be considered the contemporary "auction block" for all to see. I wanted slavery to be his shame, not mine or my ancestors'.

John Hunn was his name. I knew this from the stories my mother told.

"Your great-granddad, John Henry Freeman, worked on that farm for John Hunn," she told us.

The "farm," as she called it, was located in the lower part of Delaware on the eastern seaboard. That area in the late 1800s did not have many working plantations; instead, slaves were often indentured from one place to the next. Indentured slaves were rented out yearly and forced to work as long and hard as the slaver saw fit. In many cases they were literally worked to death.

When my mother told stories of her grandfather John Henry Freeman, she would also talk about John Hunn.

"Granddaddy said John Hunn was a good man, he was a nice man."

I secretly detested her stories. They just didn't make sense. Didn't my mother know that there were no good white people who owned slaves? She sounded like one of those howdy-do Negroes who thought that slavery was good for black people because "at least everybody was working!" But the howdy-do image never fit my mother. She was bold and black before it was popular, and proud long before James Brown told us to "say it loud."

When it came to John Hunn, the plantation owner, she was all smiles and joy.

"They were *not* slaves," she proudly declared of our ancestors. "Granddad 'worked' for the Hunn farm and stayed on as a sharecropper when slavery ended."

But I could not believe her account. I decided that she must have misunderstood, that her grandfather had tried to shield her from the harsh realities of slavery. So I could not accept what she believed to be true. How could I?

I grew up with Alex Haley's *Roots* and *The Autobiography of Miss Jane Pittman. The Autobiography of Malcolm X* was on my eleventh-grade required-reading list. I went to separate and unequal schools throughout my secondary education and was taught by the best. We were taught to be proud of who we were, to see ourselves as something more than just the descendants of slavery, and to recognize our beauty.

During the sixties and seventies, that period of "reclaiming" our identity, there was a great deal of emphasis placed on why things were the way they were. In order to find a way out of our suffering, the collective black consciousness needed to look not only at its oppression but also at its oppressors. "The white man" was a worthy culprit; it had been whites who captured, enslaved, and oppressed us. This was a fact; but that's where many have made a grand and enduring assumption by classifying one type of white man as all white men, women, and their offspring. We African Americans could be proud of our heritage even though we had been slaves because the white man had enslaved us. We could understand all of our short-comings because the white man had continuously oppressed us. Eventually we no longer needed the white man, who through the years simply became known as "whitey." Now we could be proud because we were not him. Pride is a necessary ingredient for any struggle from oppression, but too much pride comes before a fall.

Somewhere along life's journey my pride became arrogance, and arrogance gave way to exclusion. I rejected my mother's version of history without ever bothering to check out the facts. I knew that verifying her story would not be easy. I had heard these stories long before the Internet was what it is now, with its Google and search engines; long before the electronic cataloging of historical documents. But the information was still out there and I could have looked. It's what I should have done.

My refusal to accept my mother's stories as worthy of even preliminary research has created a burden that I carry now as I write. Telling this story has taken longer than it should have because I was ashamed and afraid to tell it. That old fear of being called an Oreo came back and I was worried about being seen as "not black enough." To add to my fear and shame, I did what we often do when we "stand corrected"—we lie down from fear. I have now leaned so far in the other direction that I feel the need to verify the simplest of stories.

I can hear my mother telling me from the grave, "Get to it, Bertice. Just tell it. Make it plain." So here it is, plain and simple.

John Hunn was not a slave owner. He was, as my great-grandfather said, a good man, a nice man. Even more significant (as if there needed to be more), I discovered that John Hunn was the southernmost conductor of the Underground Railroad. He was a white man, a Quaker who risked life and limb in the fight for the abolition of that most horrible institution of slavery.

How could I have missed this? How can we as a society miss the fact that there were and still are many people who fight to end oppression inside what we call "the system"?

The horrors of our history must be faced, but they must be seen in their entirety. In his 1836 book *A View of the American Slavery Question*, Elijah Porter Barrows wrote, "We are not to select isolated examples of extreme lenity or extreme cruelty and hold them up to the public as samples of the system." He was correct when he wrote this more than a century ago, and he is correct today. If we are to be truly free to govern our own movements and to be safe while we are doing so, we must look closely at the stories of our ancestors, both black and white. Only then will we find our road map to freedom from the pain of our past.

The story of John Hunn is tied to my own. In the United States, we are so intricately connected. There is no black without white, no white without black. In writing this book, I've learned that if an African American wants to find her history, she has to look through the history of white folks too. Like it or not, that's just the way it is.

I have also come to see that the searching is well worth it. There is an African proverb that says, "The way out is back through." It means that in order to find the way out of bondage and hardship, one has to retrace one's steps by going through a struggle. I had to open my heart and eyes to facts that did not conform to what I believed about the enslavement and oppression of black Americans. In order to be at peace with my existence and the struggle of my ancestors, I had to be willing to forgive those who were guilty and show gratitude to those who gave assistance.

This was a difficult task, but not nearly as difficult as the task put before black South Africans when, during the dismantling of apartheid, the Archbishop Desmond Tutu helped to create the Truth and Reconciliation Committee, whereby living victims of apartheid were asked to forgive the perpetrators of torture, murder, and oppression once those responsible publicly disclosed their deeds in detail. I often wonder if I would have been able to listen to the murderers and rapists who presented their stories to the Truth and Reconciliation Committee without wanting to exact some form of revenge as they divulged their evil deeds.

Yes, my task was great. I had to look closely at the big picture of whites and blacks, abolitionists and slaveholders, oppressed and oppressors; still, it was nothing in comparison to what the architects and participants of the Civil Rights Movement of the sixties had to do when they marched for justice and dignity and risked their life and limb for future generations.

If we look closely at the struggles of our ancestors we will find a road map to our own emotional and spiritual liberty. Our history is painful, but it is also full of hope. It sometimes evokes feelings of anger and revenge, but it should never cause shame. In discovering the truth about my personal history and the intertwined history of who John Hunn really was, I have come to see a picture of the past that liberates, forgives, and unites; this picture evokes the need to forgive and be forgiven.

There are times when history needs to be rewritten; this is a time, however, when it needs to be reexamined.

In this story, may you find your own emancipation and peace.

*Part One*

# Memory

Those who come after us seeking for information in regard to the
existence, atrocity, struggles, and destruction of slavery, will have no
trouble in finding this hydra-headed monster ruling and
tyrannizing over Church and State, North and South, white and black,
without let or hindrance, for at least several generations.
Nor will posterity have any difficulty in finding the deeds of
the brave and invincible opposers of slavery . . .
—WILLIAM STILL, 1872

ONE

# The Gift

When a person dies, a library closes.
—MANETTA GANNAWAY POLLARD

The Sankofa bird is the African expression of the phoenix mythology. It flies forward while looking backward. The female carries her egg in her mouth, representing the future of her flock.

I am the descendant of a long line of folks who have flown against the wind. My mother was a single parent to seven children, her mother was a single mother, and her mother was a child of rape. My sisters and I have all dealt with the same abuses of the women who've gone before us. We have flown in the face of abuse, incest, poverty, fear, and shame. Like most of my ancestors, I too had lost my way, my purpose.

Everything and everyone has a purpose, even our pain. I always knew that my life had a reason, but, like most black folks, I was so angry about how I got here, I had forgotten why I was here.

On the day my mother died, I received my most precious gift, the key that deciphered the code and unlocked the puzzle of pain and hardships my family endured for generations. As my eighty-seven-year-old mother lay dying in a hospital bed, sadness and fear drove me to encourage her to continue living. Through the ups and downs of life's journey, we had come to be dear friends and I couldn't stand the pain of losing anyone so precious. So as my mother told me about the legacy she would leave, I almost missed my opportunity, my key for deciphering the puzzle of my pain.

"I got something for you," she said. I had already inherited my mother's strength, and the ability to laugh through tears. I thought that was inheritance enough.

I am not certain where I picked up this belief, but I am especially attentive to the last words of a dying person. Who wouldn't be? But when a person dies, we are so consumed with life that we pay little attention to those "last lessons."

In the film *Signs*, M. Night Shyamalan weaves the theme of "last lessons" throughout his story, while waiting until the very end to reveal its full meaning. As inquisitive as I've been about the dying words of others, in the moment of my mother's death, I was not in tune. I listened for ways to give comfort but had a difficult time focusing on the lesson. She was up to her old trick of pulling me into a joke I'd heard hundreds of times before.

When I was a child, my mother, burdened with seven children and the irony of being both poor and proud, would often make games out of our struggle.

"We're having something special for dinner," she'd say, with mock laughter.

"Poke rolls and grits. Poke your mouth out, roll your eyes, and grit your teeth, 'cause that's all you getting."

My six brothers and sisters and I knew this meant we were having beans, but the thought that it could have meant no food at all made the beans taste so much better. We lived in a three-bedroom house on Gordon Street in Wilmington, Delaware. Gordon Street was more of an alley than a street. Wedged between two numbered blocks, it had once been a storage area for the old water station nearby. The street was lined on both sides with lime-green garages, which back in the sixties housed the belongings of those who could afford to store things someplace outside their homes. In the middle of that block were number 4 and number 6 Gordon Street. Initially we lived in number 4, and then moved "up" to number 6. The homes were modest places and old even for the area. The streets of Wilmington are lined now with houses familiar to cities like Baltimore and Philadelphia. Unlike their New York brownstone cousins, the row houses of Wilmington are close to the ground with small porches. The oldest of these homes are on Market Street, the city's main street, and the racial dividing line of the fifties and sixties. They are made of stone. A few of them, now historical landmarks, lead to actual underground tunnels where runaways who had been enslaved would find shelter and eventually freedom. Ours was not a historical landmark; it was just old.

Our house was still heated by a coal-burning furnace, which made life even harder, given the fact that we could barely afford coal. We often sat shivering as favorite pieces of furniture became much-needed wood for the furnace.

We were cold and poor, but somehow there was laughter. Alice Walker once wrote, "There is a point at which even grief becomes absurd. At that point, laughter gushes up to retrieve the sanity." The laughter in our house was the sanity-retrieving kind.

My mother finally did learn to laugh without the sorrow, and she kept right on laughing, right up until the day she died, when she said, "I got something for you," through smiling eyes and short, labored breaths. "Poke rolls and grits." She laughed as best as she could. "Just kidding," she said. "I have been lying here in this hospital for a week trying to figure out what I can give you, and now I know."

I tried to protest, but she wasn't having it.

"Mom, you don't have to give me anything. You gave me life and that's enough."

I'd made this same statement many times during our last fifteen years together. She had moved in with me and we became the best of friends. My childhood with her had been difficult, but my mother taught me to forgive and let go of the past; not an easy feat considering the fact that she was the one I needed to forgive the most.

Poverty can make you mean. When we were growing up we were really poor, so at times my mother was really mean. She worked at a nursing home for most of my childhood.

Layton Home for the Elderly was a thirty-minute walk from our house. We didn't have a car and bus fare was more than my mother could afford, so she walked in the heat and in the snow in shoes that were lined with newspaper. To make ends meet, she pulled double shifts. She had to bathe, feed, and carry patients from one room to the next who were often verbally and physically abusive. She once came home smelling of the feces and urine that had been thrown at her.

"I tried to clean it off," she said, "but some things run deep."

All day long she'd duck and dodge the name-calling that often accompanied Alzheimer's and other forms of dementia. So at night, my mother drank.

She tried to drink away the pain of the abuse and of her loneliness. She drank to escape the pain of her childhood and the sufferings of poverty.

I came to recognize the spiraling stages the alcohol took her through.

Stage one—the sickly sweet "I love you" stage: "You kids mean the world to me. I wish I could do more for you."

Stage two—the "sick and tired of being sick and tired" stage: "I'm so tired, I don't know what to do."

Stage three—the "you don't know" stage: "Y'all don't know what I go through. You sure enough don't care."

Stage four—the "I wish you were never born" stage: "I can't stand the sight of you . . . you make me sick to my stomach."

Stage five—the "what's been done to me will be done to you" stage: "You black bitch, whore, I hate you. Get the belt."

I understand now how painful these stages had to be for my mother, but back then, I felt only the pain she put on me.

Then, when my mother was in her late sixties, she suddenly stopped drinking. For most people the detox process is slow and long, with several false starts before they can finally introduce themselves at a meeting with "Hello, my name is _____ and I've been sober for _____ days." My mother didn't attend any sobriety programs; one day she simply decided to stop drinking. By then I was finishing my doctoral work. Before that time, I rarely went home for visits; they were just too painful. The memories of growing up in an alcoholic home always came rushing back whenever I saw my mother with a glass in her hand.

Just before I completed my doctoral work I received a letter from my mother saying that she wanted to talk with me. In her note she said that she had been doing a lot of soul-searching and had made some changes. When I called, I was surprised to hear the voice on the other end of the phone. Prior to that time, I never knew which of her stages she would be in. Sometimes her voice would be sweet with praise; at others she would slur bitter insults, telling me that I thought my education made me believe I was better than everybody else. But that day when we talked on the phone, my mother's voice was crystal clear and carried a wisdom I had not heard before. She said she had news for me.

"What is it?" I asked.

"Well," she said after a short pause that felt much longer, "I don't know if you will believe this, but I have stopped drinking."

I heard my mother's words, but had a hard time taking them in; the day that I had prayed long and hard for had come, and I did not know what to say.

"You there, Bessie?" my mother said, calling me by my middle name. It was not until I had a doctoral degree that my family began to call me Bertice, my first name, the one everyone else knew me by.

"I'm here, Mom. I'm just surprised." My tears were already flowing. I remembered back to when my mother would beat me for pouring out her liquor, the liquor that I believed was the source of all our problems.

"I'm really happy for you" was all I could manage. My short response did nothing to dampen my mother's spirits. She had stepped away from her old self and was coming back to the person she was meant to be.

"I know I put you through a lot, but I'm asking you to forgive me," she said.

I mumbled something about how I had already forgiven her, but it was really just lip service. I had prayed and waited for that day, but when it finally came, I wasn't really ready. I still harbored resentment and anger. My Christianity went only so far. I could love and help others in need, but I was having a hard time forgiving my mother. The pain of my childhood still lingered and I had not yet learned how to truly forgive.

We talked a bit longer and I agreed to visit her when I had the time and money. It was several more months before I finally did get back to Delaware, and when I did, I could see that my mother had indeed changed. I asked her how she stopped drinking.

"I asked God to help me," she said, "and God did." For my mother it was that simple. Her decision to stop drinking was sometimes hard, but most of the time it wasn't, because, as she said, "it was something that I knew I needed to do."

In time, I learned to forgive her for the past. She made it easy because she was full of love and laughter. Once my mother stopped drinking, she spent most of every day of her life in joy and gratitude, and she tried hard to make up for any wrongs she had committed.

Later, when she moved to California to live with me, she would try to give me money to "help out," but I always refused it.

"Mom, you know I don't need your money," I'd say, being prideful.

"Bertice, you can't always be the giver," she'd say, ignoring my ignorance. "Sooner or later, you are going to have to learn to take. Life is all about balance."

"Well," she said on the day she died, "I don't have a lot of money."

"I know, Mommy, that's all right." I was trying hard to be calm for her, trying hard to hold back my tears and regrets. On the days leading up to this one, my mother had expressed her fears.

"I'm not ready to go yet, I'm scared," she'd said.

I repeated what I had said over the previous two years while she suffered one serious illness after another.

"You'll be fine, Mommy, just believe," I'd said to her time after time.

She believed and she was fine. Her physicians called her the miracle lady. In just two years, she'd suffered a brain tumor, five heart attacks, and six strokes. Amazingly, there was no neurological damage. So, after long stays in the hospital, most of which were spent in intensive care, she'd leave the hospital smiling and laughing.

"If y'all want to see me again, you'd better come to my house, 'cause I'm out of here," she'd say to the hospital staff.

The staff all had a thing for my mother, but who wouldn't have? She was joyful during that time, even when she was in pain.

On their days off, the staff members would come around to see her and would spend the afternoon listening to her encourage them to keep on keeping on. She'd have me bring in extra-large Hershey bars, which she used to "prop up the night-shift nurses." Even the physicians, who had little extra time while they did their rounds, would pull up a chair to spend time with her. She would tease, correct, encourage, and nurture everyone who walked into her room.

"You need to smile or go home," my mother told one specialist. The physician introduced himself and told my mother his specialty. "I know you're special," she said, "but that don't mean you can't smile. When you smile, no one will know that you are in pain."

The man bowed his head and thanked her. From that day on, he came in with a smile. "Is this good, Ms. Berry?" he'd ask, grinning.

"That's just fine," she would say.

If a staff member asked, "How are you?" without seeming to really want to know, my mother would ask, "What do you think? Y'all done probed me from the rootie to the tootie. How would you be doing?" Then she'd smile and say, "I'm probably better than you since you have to put up with me."

For the two years that my mother was in and out of the hospital, she mustered up the strength to be pleasant and kind. But at the end, when she contracted pneumonia and couldn't get well, she became fearful and frail.

The country-and-western singer Rob Conroy had already

written my mother's heart-song. She was "Tired of Living and Too Afraid of Dying."

I had been praying with her and for her. I asked God to heal and restore her. I would pray for hours on end. My mother would smile and listen. She would even say "Amen" and "Yes, Lord," in all the right places. Then, after I'd finish, she would pray the same short prayer she had been saying for years: "Divine Love always has and always will supply our every need. So let nothing hinder or delay the Divine Plan that the Creator has for your life today. We are moving on and on and on."

One day, when she was particularly low, I decided to pray her prayer for her. "I don't know," she said after I finished. Her eyes were fearful and full of tears. "I'm scared."

Until then, I hadn't paid much attention to my mother's prayer. I'd heard it thousands of times, but I decided that it was a bit too New Agey for my fundamentalist beliefs, though I went along with it to please her. But the day I prayed her prayer for her I began to hear the meaning behind the words. "God," or "Divine Love," as my mother called it, had supplied our every need. My childhood had been framed in poverty—very rarely did we get the things we wanted—but as my mother said, our basic needs had been met. I could see that there had been a plan for my life that included all of the things I had gone through. Somehow, some way, I was moving forward.

I wondered where the prayer came from, so I asked her. She said that she didn't remember, that it was just something they all used to say. I knew that "they all" meant her older kinfolks, but there weren't any of them left. I needed to know more and had a sense of urgency about finding the source of her prayer. If I could find some information about it, my mother could find the peace she needed. That night I did a computer search and immediately found the prayer's origins. The absolute best use of modern technology happens when it connects our present condition to our past history.

I was amazed to find that the prayer had come from Mary Baker Eddy, the founder of the Christian Science Movement. Ms. Baker developed the philosophy of Christian Science while struggling with a lifelong illness. Throughout her youth, Ms. Baker had gone from one faith healer to the next, when she decided to decipher what she called the science of Christ.

I must admit right here and now that I was one of those overeducated folks who, because of all their learning, had somehow come to believe that old folks live only by their wits and rarely come in contact with radical thinking. I now know better. It makes perfect sense that an eighty-seven-year-old black woman would come in contact with philosophical thinking; she had learned to take the time to think.

The words on my computer screen eloquently expressed what my mother had said for years, that "God ain't never want nobody to suffer and Divine Love supplies everything we need."

My mother's ideas were right there in print in a letter that Mary Baker Eddy had written to a follower who had been questioning his calling:

*The place you seek is seeking you. The place you need is need-*
*ing you. Divine Principle brings need and supply together for*
*mutual good. God wisely, intelligently and lovingly controls,*
*guides, protects, prospers and blesses the union of man and his*
*[purpose].*

*All that you need to do is to see that your consciousness is*
*fully prepared, enlarged, uplifted, joyous, expectant of infinite*
*good, so that no sense of limitation may hinder the manifesta-*
*tion of God's will for you. You know that God's will for you is*
*perfection, nothing less. All we need ever to change is our sense*
*of discord to the consciousness of harmony . . .*

I copied these words and a meditation from Mary Baker
Eddy and read them the next day to my mother. When I'd finished, I looked up and saw her smiling again. The color had
come back to her face and she was her old bold self. I thought
that everything would be okay and that she'd once again amaze
the doctors with another of her miraculous recoveries. She began to laugh and clap her hands as she often did whenever she
had figured something out.

"You all right, Mommy?" I asked.

"I remember now, I remember," she said joyfully. "Everything is clear and good."

My mother died two hours later, but before she did, she
gave me the gift I needed the most. It was the key to unlocking
a memory, which led to my redemption.

"I got something for you," she had said. "I don't have a lot of money, and all the good jewelry I have, you gave me. I don't think it would be right for me to give it back," she said, laughing. "I got poke rolls and grits. Ha-ha, just kidding."

By now I knew that my mother was in tremendous pain. The nurses had tried over and over again to find a vein so they could run a PICC (peripherally inserted central catheter) line, an internal IV. She was still laughing and smiling right through her pain.

"I have figured out what you need the most," she said, eyes sparkling. "I want you to share this with anybody who needs it," she continued. "Give it to the ones who are always trying to make a way for somebody else, 'cause the ones who are trying to make a way need to find their own way too."

I was saddened by the fact that my mother, who for most of her life had few material possessions, was still trying to give me something while she was in such pain. The sadness brought shame and I lost focus on the tremendous gift.

Pain can make you forget so much that you lose your way. By then I could see that my mother really was slipping away. In Elizabeth Kübler-Ross's *On Death and Dying*, passages of grieving are outlined. She points out that denial, the first stage, happens when a loved one dies and the living have a hard time accepting it. Well, I had an even more difficult time believing that my mother was going to die. Her strength and resilience made her seem invincible. She was only eighty-seven and I was certain that she'd hang around to see one hundred. I was numb from regret for all the years I wasted being angry with her. Once she made her transformation, and I could see her true self, I wondered why I had missed the obvious fact that she was an incredible woman.

As I stood at my mother's bedside on her last day on earth, I was sorry for all that I had not done with her. The past fifteen years had been wonderful; she had lived with me. We would take road trips or go "exploring," as she called it, looking at God's everyday beauty. My mother was proud of all her children, but because she lived with me, I was able to get the daily doses of encouragement and praise. She'd wake up singing, and from the time she came downstairs for breakfast until she went to bed at night, she would let me know what an incredible daughter I was.

Now I wondered if I had been as good to her as she'd been to me. I was so caught up in my own pain, I could barely hear what she was telling me. "Pain is temporary, peace is eternal, just keep on living," she said. When my mother passed away, I experienced a pain that was deeper than any sorrow I'd ever known, but with that pain came my greatest joy. In *Redemption Song* I had written that "Joy comes for those who suffer, that peace comes for those who are in pain."

On the day of my mother's passing, and for many days that followed, I came to understand the full meaning of those words. I knew for certain that true joy can be felt only after real suffering. I understand why pain is the price for peace.

When my mother left this earth, she left behind her greatest gift.

"I know just what y'all need," she said again, smiling. "I figured it out. I'm leaving, but I'm taking all of our past hurts and shame and I'm packing them up. I'm taking that bag with me to the other side. You got a clean slate, and y'all are going to be free."

Just before she "gave up the ghost," as she and the old folks used to say, I asked her for one more thing.

"Help me write this book, Mommy," I said, through loneliness and tears. Seconds later, she left her body, moving on to Oneness, to Peace, to Divine Love.

When she died that day, she was smiling and she was at peace.

Freedom is the ability to govern one's own movement, physically, emotionally, spiritually, and mentally. My mother's decision to pack up the pains of her life and of our ancestral past and to take them with her to the other side was the beginning of my journey toward true freedom.

I know for certain that, as Iona said in my novel *Redemption Song*, "freedom ain't just about getting free, it's about being free then turning around and setting somebody else free. But the chains on your wrists ain't as strong as the ones on our minds. The only thing that can win over the evil [of enslavement] is when we learn to love and strive to love, 'cause we ain't got time for nothing else."

I used my mother's gift of a clean slate to start this journey. With love I have retraced my family's steps and have found the road to freedom.

# TWO

# Pain Before Beauty

The heart knows its own bitterness, and no stranger shares its joy.

—PROVERBS 14:10

There is an ancient proverb that says, "When the student is ready, the teacher appears." I believe this to be true. I have also come to see that when the student is not ready the teacher appears and reappears until she is ready to listen.

This was the case for me. But life has a way of slowing you down until you are willing to listen and learn. In 2004, when my mother first became ill, I had recently gotten married. This was the second marriage for me. The first ended after only a few years; this one would not survive that long. My sister Christine once said that she didn't believe we Berrys were meant to be married. She felt that my mother's children were all born to be as free as birds, settling down just long enough for the season to change. "Then," she said, "we should build a new nest in a new part of the world."

I didn't like the idea of being as free as a bird. I wanted to give my love to one person and to spend the rest of my life with him. I'd grown up in the shadow of my mother's loneliness and had decided that the single life was not for me. My mother had seven children by seven different men.

She once told me that she would never stay in a bad relationship, not even for a child. If a relationship went bad, she left, sometimes before the father even knew she was pregnant.

When I was a girl, I longed for a father figure, someone to look up to. Back in the sixties my friends all had fathers. They weren't all good, but they were all there. The stereotypical household of the single black mother had not been thought of, nor had it been typed into the stereo of our minds. I never knew my father, and until I was thirty, I didn't even know who he was. My ideas of love and family were formed by the families that lived around me and the ones I'd gone to church with.

My first marriage happened right out of graduate school. I was twenty-six and had just earned my doctoral degree in sociology. He asked, I said yes, and we got married. It happened quickly and was over even quicker. I did not look back, I had no regrets, nor did I dwell on the failure. But when I married again in 2004, I vowed in my heart and my head that it would be forever.

I needed my marriage to last forever. I was running away from my own past and the past of my ancestors. I did not want to be a single mother like my mother, nor did I want to be the free bird that my sister described.

But life has a way of handing you just what you need when you think you don't need it. Back when I was in graduate school, I stayed focused on my goal. I did not date the entire time I was in college. I was too afraid that some family curse would catch me and take me back to the cycles of poverty and abuse that I had crawled out of. If a young man asked me out, I'd politely refuse.

Once, when I was near the end of my doctoral program and my guard was way down, a young man who I thought was a friend asked if we could at least study together. I'd previously refused his offers for dinner dates, so he tried another course of action.

I am not one for dwelling on the past, nor do I ever want to be identified by the bad things that happened to me, so I will tell this quickly. That way we can move right on to the healing. I have never revealed this to a soul, but the soul can bear a burden for only so long.

I was raped.

For weeks I hid inside my apartment and myself trying to wonder what I had done wrong. My guilt and fear manifested themselves into a false pregnancy. I was afraid that I would end up back in the poverty of where I had come from. After weeks of fretting, I finally went to an abortion clinic. Now, before I go any further, I need to tell you that I grew up in the Pentecostal Church. One day in school, when I was twelve years old, for no apparent reason, I had begun to cry. When the teacher asked me why, I cried some more. I know now that the pressures of my little life had weighed me down, but back then, I just told the teacher that I didn't know why I was crying. I had few friends and no adults I could tell my troubles to.

This was way before school therapists, or after-school television "specials" (the ones that gave out 800 numbers). The teacher asked if I wanted to talk about my crying, but I just said no. He was bright enough to let go of the subject without dropping it entirely.

"Bertice," he said one day during lunch break, "I never see you playing with anybody. Who would you say is your best friend?" he asked.

Well, he was right. I didn't have any friends. Between school and the cleaning jobs I did to help out with household bills, I had no time for the silliness of childhood. I looked around the room, trying to find someone I could call a friend. Out of somewhere special (I used to say "out of nowhere," but I know better now), the name Barbara popped into my head. Barbara Dorsey was the quietest girl in our class. I had no friends, but at least I talked. That day, I picked Barbara because she was friendless like me.

Even now when I see someone with a beautiful gap between

her front teeth, I smile and think of Barbara. Well, after lunch break had ended and we were back in class, my teacher told Barbara and me to go out in the hallway and figure out why I was crying. When we did, nothing came to mind, and Barbara, bless her young heart, never asked. She managed to speak only once that day.

"Do you want to go to church with me?" she said in her tiny voice. I immediately said yes. My family had gone to church back when I was much younger. We stayed until I was about six. That's when my mother started to drink. I found out when I was much older that because she had so many kids by as many men, the church folks had labeled her a harlot. The pressure my mother felt because she did not fit the proper image of "church folks" became shame and the shame grew into guilt. She left the church, and hated it when I went back.

I loved the music and the chaotic way the Holy Spirit was allowed to take over. When Barbara asked me if I wanted to go, I saw it as an escape.

The church was about a mile from my house but I would walk it each Sunday and five nights a week. I would go after my cleaning job in the evenings. My mother never expressed worry or concern over the fact that I was not at home. Her concern lay somewhere in the fact that her daughter had given her life over to the same church folks who had rejected her.

"I know they up in that church talking about me. All them folks think they so holy. They ain't shit and neither are you," she would say.

Her drunken accusations made me cling to the church even more. Whenever there was an altar call for secret prayer requests, I would go up and pray for my mother and for myself.

"Please, God, let my mother turn her life around and please, God, let me get out of that house. And if it's your will, Jesus, let me go to college."

Just in case that was not enough, at night I would also wish on the stars that I would go to college. I had been told by one of the church mothers, an older woman, that I was not really pretty enough to get a good man, so I should try to study hard so that I would be able to take care of myself. Today, I have come to see myself as beautiful, but I'm so glad that back then I believed what she'd said.

In some ways my church life was very similar to my home life. Both were loud and filled with frenetic energy; each espoused great truths while at the same time telling evil lies.

At home, I'd hear my mother say, "One day things will get better." Later on that evening, after the alcohol had taken hold, she would declare that nothing was ever going to change.

At church, I'd hear my brilliant pastor share the words of Proverbs that "wisdom is the principal thing, so we should get wisdom, but when we did, we must also get an understanding." Shortly afterward, someone would testify about how the devil was always on his back and that he would never get ahead. Somewhere in the midst of that up and down, I chose to be up. I believed that I could work my way out of poverty and shame and I had learned to do just that. That is, until I got raped.

My fear could not match the guilt I heaped upon myself. Going for an abortion was not something a good "saved" girl did. It did not matter that I was raped, because I believed that I had caused that too.

I lived and went to graduate school in a small town, so I knew many of the other women who sat waiting to see the one doctor at the clinic. I had to walk past a man who walked back and forth carrying a sign that declared that I and the other women were sinners for murdering our unborn babies. I wanted to tell him that I was not like the other women. I wanted to tell him that I was saved and filled with the Holy Spirit. As I got closer to the door of the clinic I suddenly realized that I was just like every woman there. And that no one had the right to judge another woman's story.

I sat in the clinic afraid, and wondered what I had done to deserve this. I had worked hard and had been focused, but still got caught in the cycle I had feared most, being single and pregnant.

When it was my turn to see the doctor, I was told that I had experienced a false pregnancy. The doctor also chastised me, saying that abortion was not a form of birth control and that I should plan parenthood, not fall into it. I began to cry and I told him my story. At first he looked as though he had heard the "I was raped" excuse one time too many, but when I told him that I was near the end of my doctoral program and had been a virgin, he softened. He held my hand and said he was sorry about what had happened to me.

"Finish your program and do good things," he said.

"I will" was all I could manage.

On my way out, the man with the picket sign screamed at me, "Your baby is crying out from the grave, you murderer."

I cried and walked away.

That night, I vowed that I would never get pregnant, and that I could not be anybody's mother.

Life sure is funny. The thing we fear most will always happen. That's because we spend so much of our energy fearing it. Shortly after the divorce from my first husband, my mother informed me that my sister's children were in danger of being put into foster care. The youngest, a three-month-old girl, had been born crack-addicted, like her two brothers. The children moved in with me. Later they were joined by others from similar backgrounds, and over the past fifteen years, I, like my mother, have been a single parent.

When I got married the second time, I did it for my children. True, I felt that they needed a father, but my mother had become ill and life came rushing back in on me. My husband and I were having all the difficulties of a new marriage and he was trying hard to adjust to the changes that came with marrying into a large family. My mother's illness took precedence over his needs and our marriage ended. But I still had my mother and I still had my children to comfort me. I could truly see the blessing that comes when you carry a burden, and I began to understand how my mother could curse her children one day and praise them the next.

When the doctors found the tumor on her brain, I knew that my focus and energy had to be centered on her wellness. The more I focused on her, the more difficulty I had in my marriage. I tried hard to handle everything but eventually gave up on the marriage.

"I didn't think it was going to work anyway," my mother said after I waved my flag of defeat.

I asked her why she had let me go through it in the first place, and she laughed and said, "'Cause you hadn't struggled enough."

I thought my mother's medications were getting the best of her or that the tumor was causing her to say crazy things.

"Why would you say that?" I asked anyway.

That's when my mother told me that she believed I had been called to do a major work, but I needed to go through something before I could do it.

It really is the tumor, I thought to myself.

My mother's illness had truly taken its toll. She had been active her entire life; this was only the second time she had been slowed down by an illness or injury. She was eighty-five then, and prior to the brain tumor, the only other hospital stays had been to give birth and to have back surgery. The heavy lifting of aging patients had taken its toll on her physical health, but had not slowed her down. After back surgery, she left the hospital and went right back to work at the nursing home.

This time, the hospital stays lasted for several weeks at a

time and continued over a two-year period. I spent most of those nights with her at the hospital because I did not want her to be alone.

Hospital time can be difficult for anyone, but for my mother it was grueling. She wanted to be at home with me and her grandkids and her laundry. She loved doing laundry. We often laughed at the fact that laundry was her hobby. We never sent clothes to the cleaners, even when the instructions said "Dry-clean only." My mother believed that all clothes could be cleaned at home either in a good washing machine or by hand.

I did not inherit her love for doing laundry and would often joke that the desire to do it skips a generation.

My mother longed to get back to "*her* washing machine," as she called it. "I got to clean that sweater," she said, looking at the one I had been wearing for a week.

I had been spending the nights with my mother in the hospital and went home only to shower, check on my children, and prepare dinners for them. My clothing was the last thing on my mind, but it was one of her major concerns. She once told me that she grew to love doing laundry because it was one of the only things she could give us that seemed almost new. I asked her what she meant and she said that since she could barely afford to buy new clothes, she could at least keep the ones we had clean. Making our secondhand clothes soft and beautiful gave her a sense of joy. The ability to find peace in poverty is an amazing thing.

My mother wanted to get out of the hospital but couldn't, so I tried to entertain her as best as I could. On all of her hospital stays she was in a private room. She received Medicare, which covered a great deal since she had hardly been sick before, and what it didn't cover, I paid for. So after every heart attack or every stroke she'd leave the emergency room for ICU and then was wheeled to a private room.

"Thank God," she'd say. "I have the room to myself. When you and Jeanine come in to read to me, we won't bother anybody."

Jeanine was my business manager of ten years and became my mother's "other daughter." We would take turns "reading and running," as we came to call those hospital stays.

"You all are either reading or running," a nurse remarked after seeing Jeanine and I leave to pick up children, do chores, or catch a flight for one of my corporate lectures. "Reading and running; you two are always busy," she said.

My mother, who dropped out of school in the ninth grade, loved to read. A year before the doctors found the brain tumor, her eyesight went bad and we feared that, like her mother, she would eventually go blind. Fortunately, my mother was a good candidate for artificial lens implants, which saved her eyesight.

"God is good and science done come a long way," my mother said after her surgery. She was elated by everything she saw.

"I can even see the cracks in the sidewalk," she exclaimed

a few days after the surgery. Before then, she never bothered to tell me that she was having a hard time seeing. One day, I noticed that she was holding a bottle of vanilla extract extremely close to her face.

"What's wrong, Mom?" I asked.

"Oh, I'm just making sure this is vanilla and not almond extract," she told me. I immediately knew that something was wrong. We went to the doctor right away, and soon afterward we went to the surgeon to prepare for the operation.

"Any later would have been too late," the surgeon said.

Weeks later, when my mother's eyesight was good again, I asked her why she hadn't told me that she could barely see.

"I didn't want to bother you," she said. "You take care of so much, I just didn't want to be a burden."

I was sad that my mother felt that way, but I tried not to show it. I laughed and sarcastically told her that not telling was the right thing to do since a blind old woman would have been easier to live with than a sighted one. We both laughed and she again told me how proud I made her.

After her eye surgery my mother went back to "really reading." For some time, she'd gone through the motions of reading, so no one would know that she couldn't see. She loved to read and would read whatever books I did. When she was sick and in the hospital, Jeanine and I would read to her so she could relax and "see the story," as she called it. Still, she didn't like to bother anyone, so she was always glad when she got a room to herself. I would read her the paper and novels until she got tired and then I'd turn on the television. It served as the background noise that enabled her to feel like everything else in the world was still the same.

The last years of my mother's life were also her best years. She'd been diagnosed with a brain tumor but our relationship was the best it had been. The years of drinking and abuse were behind us and we were free to focus on the things that really mattered. For my mother, it was mending the relationships with her children. For me, it was making sure she had whatever she needed.

My mother didn't need much. If you asked her what she wanted, she'd talk about her children and grandchildren. She wanted to know that everybody was okay.

"If you could send a couple of dollars to your sister, that would be good," she'd say.

Her own personal needs could be met with a good book, fried chicken, Hershey's chocolate, and an episode of the TV show *Bonanza*. I've always marveled at the love that older folks have for Westerns. I have never been a fan.

One night, after she had fallen asleep in the hospital during one of her longer stays, and I was free to change the channel from her seemingly endless hours of *Bonanza* episodes, I found a PBS documentary on the abolitionist movement. The program focused on the many acts of bravery that occurred during slavery. It told the story of the fearless rebels who fought to end slavery and gave aid to fugitive runaways. I heard the familiar names of Harriet Tubman and William Lloyd

Garrison, of Nat Turner and John Brown. I had heard all these names before.

Then I heard the name John Hunn. I sat up in the hospital chair that doubled as a bed and a shiver went down my spine. It was the feeling you get when, as the old folks say, "somebody walked over your grave." Right then I knew that the old folks had gotten this one wrong; no one was walking over my burial place; I was the one doing the grave walking.

"John Hunn," I said out loud. When I did, my mother sprang to.

"What is it?" she asked.

"They were talking about John Hunn on TV," I told her. "They said he was from Delaware and that he was an abolition-ist."

"Uh-huh," my mother said, smiling, "I told you he was an abolitionist. I told you that he and your great-granddaddy used to help folks get to freedom," she said.

I was shocked and annoyed. The name I had heard so many times before was coming from the television set and had been included in the abolitionist movement.

"But that's the man who owned the plantation our family lived on," I told my mother. "The one whose name I used in *Redemption Song*. He owned the plantation our family lived on when they were slaves," I said. "You never said anything about him being an abolitionist."

My mother smiled a "you think you know everything" smile, the smile she reserved before launching into one of her history lessons.

She was a great storyteller. I learned later on that this was a trait she picked up from her grandfather, one she passed on to me and my siblings. She loved to tell her version of history—the history she saw and heard for herself. She enjoyed helping my kids with social studies projects.

"Put that computer thing away," she would say. "Y'all don't need no World Wide Web to find out about Amelia Earhart. I was there. I remember how we used to sit around the radio at night waiting to hear the latest update on where she was. Then, when they lost her, oh Lord, it was like we lost a family member."

My mother could truly bring history to life. Why not? She had been around for eighty-five years and remembered almost everything.

"Bertice, if I told you once, I told you twice, John Hunn did not own slaves," she said that day in the hospital.

I tried to argue what I knew would be a lost cause. I tried to point out to my mother that she had never said that John Hunn was an abolitionist; all she ever told us was that he was nice and that he owned the "farm" our family lived on.

"I told you he was a good man," she scoffed. "Don't make me get up," she continued, only half-joking. "I'll still beat the black off of you."

It's a wonderful thing when life evolves so far that the words that once caused you fear can eventually bring laughter. When I was a child, my mother thought that corporal punishment was her God-given right. She beat us for any reason with any object, and would add insult to injury by saying, "I could

kill you, bury you out back, and make another one that looks
just like you."

Later in life, she admitted that she'd been wrong, and
wished she could have taken it all back.

"Folks beat their kids 'cause they've been beaten and they
still haven't learned no other way. But it's wrong. With all the
education and the money in the world, you'd think that somebody would come up with a better way to set children on the
right path."

Whenever she got on this horse (that for me sat mighty
high), I'd silently wonder, What took you so long? Why couldn't
you figure this out before, back when you were beating us?

We laughed about my mother's old promises of a beating
until she looked at me and said again, "If you would have listened to me about John Hunn, you could have learned the
truth. He did not own slaves," she said with all the pride she
could muster. "You got all them degrees, but you don't listen."

"Okay, Mom, who was he?" I asked.

My mother then shared with me information that had escaped me, and others like me, for too long. As she said, it's not
like she hadn't told me these stories before; it's just that I
wasn't listening. The history of slavery in America is a painful
one, and, as I've already pointed out, pain can cause you to forget the truth.

I have always been fascinated by black history. I am proud
of who I am and my heritage. But oppression brings shame,
and too often we try to remedy shame with blame, which re-
sults only in animosity.

The "Black is Beautiful" movement of the sixties was an attempt to replace the shame of the residue of slavery with pride and the awareness that contemporary black people are descendants of enslaved Africans. We all wanted to believe that we were the great-great-descendant of someone great. We wanted to believe we were all warriors and kings, and we were beautiful. As far as we were concerned back then, had it not been for evil white slave traders, today we would have tremendous wealth and would be happy and free.

Belief in the "evil slave owner" served many African Americans well and ignited our path to middle-class citizenry, but this one-sided perspective got in the way of the whole picture, a picture that provided a more balanced representation of what lay in our past (individually and collectively) and would lead us beyond the middle class into the realm of all possibilities.

That night, I could not sleep; I could not stop wondering how I had not known of my family's connections to the abolitionist movement. I wondered how I could have been, as my mother often said, "so bright and yet so dumb." I thought about how wrong I'd been when I used the Hunn name to represent the evil slaveholder in my book *Redemption Song*.

As I sat in my mother's hospital room that evening, somewhere between my mental ramblings and the nurses' rounds I resolved to find out more about the life of John Hunn and of my great-grandfather, John Henry Freeman, and about the ties that bound them together. There in that room, the place that would later be the hospital where she died, I was reborn into the beginning of a truth that would help set me free. The story of the ties between blacks and whites during slavery is a story that has not been fully told. When we think of slavery, we rarely think of the brave white stationmasters, the white revolutionaries, or the white conductors of the Underground Railroad. Rarely do we picture the simple, everyday people, both black and white, who stood on the side of right. When I found John Hunn and John Henry Freeman I got an entirely different picture of the history of slavery, one that can liberate me and others from the pains of our past.

# THREE

# *Burdens Down, Lord, Burdens Down*

The Negro is the lord of sound.

—ZORA NEALE HURSTON

When I was five years old, my mother abruptly stopped going to church. I can remember the last day we went as a family. My brother Kevin and I were supposed to sing a duet. It was late in the year, but we were wearing the outfits we'd gotten for Easter. My brother wore a red blazer with a gold emblem on the pocket. His navy blue pants were creased to perfection. I had on a light wool dress, with cream, pink, and green blocks. My hair was pulled into the three simple plaits that most black girls wore back then. I had on my favorite shoes, black patent leather flats with a thin strap and a white pearl button on the side. We were "sharp as a tack," my mother had said.

We'd practiced our song for days. I was so happy.

"I feel better, so much better, since I laid my burdens down." I sang it loudly all week long. My brother Kevin, who is ten months older than me, would chime in, "Glory, glory, glory hallelujah," and I would shout, "Hallelujah, halle- lujah."

Our duet was going to be perfect. But when the minister called us up to sing, Kevin would not get out of his seat.

"I don't want to," he cried.

Kevin sat there, tears streaming down his Vaselined face. My mother believed in the powers of Vaseline petroleum jelly. We used it for everything from skin moisturizer to shoe polish. Kevin sat there crying while I marched right to the front of the church and sang without him. My mother smiled with pride and after church all the members came up to me and said how great I was. My mother was so happy. It felt good to make her happy.

The following Sunday, I got up in anticipation of going to church. I looked forward to hearing compliments and seeing my mother smile again, but it was not to be. My mother said we weren't going. I didn't understand.

"Why?" I asked.

"Because I said so" was her reply.

There was something in the way she said it that made me

know that I had better not ask again. It would be more than thirty years before we would go to church as a family again.

Time went by and my mother began to drink. As with any addiction, it started slowly and gradually. She'd have a drink on Tuesday, then again on Friday. Soon my mother was drinking every night. The more she drank, the madder she got. My oldest sister, Myrna, had moved away to New York, so Christine was left to look after us. Christine dropped out of school in the ninth grade. It was a terrible shame, because she really loved school. She had dreams of becoming an anthropologist. She learned about anthropology in school and decided that someday she would travel and dig up the history that black people had created around the world. There is always hope. My sister Christine is now sixty-three years old and has just enrolled in college.

Back then there was little money for things like food or electricity; there was certainly no time or money for Christine to go to college.

My mother had very little income to show for the hard and long hours she worked. She had been thrust into a series of painful experiences, and then there were the men. When I hear people talk negatively about women who have had children by more than one man, I know that they don't understand that for many of these women, the men who fathered their children were the only men they had planned to be with. In their hearts and minds, each one was to be the last.

My mother longed for the family life she'd had back on the

farm where she grew up, played, and had meals that came from the land that she lived on in the southern part of Delaware. Going to church had been my mother's way of getting the sense of community she longed for.

Years later, I found out why my mother left the church. One of the visiting ministers had been seeing my mother. When she and the other members found out that the man was married, all of them, including her pastor, decided that she must have done something to cause him to stray; after all, she was the one with "all them kids, by all them different men."

My mother didn't share this with me until years later, when I had to confide in her that my pastor had been making passes at me.

"That's it," she yelled. "The enemy has been using church to keep folks from God for too long."

Then she told me what happened to her years before. As she was talking to me I could see myself singing the song I'd sung that day in church when I was five: "I feel better, so much better, since I laid my burdens down."

The church has always been an integral part of the lives of African Americans. In her book *African American Spirituality, Thought and Culture*, Phyllis Baker, Ph.D., points out that "African Americans are descendants of spiritual zealots whose entire existence and survival were based on the interaction of spiritual and mystical forces. These forces are believed to be responsible for prosperity and poverty, sickness and health, freedom and bondage and every other conceivable aspect of life." Blacks in Delaware are especially tied to church life. In fact, the oldest black church in the country was chartered in Delaware in 1813 by former slave Peter Spencer, of the Union Church of Africans. Spencer started the first independent black denomination, known today as AUMP, or African Union First Colored Methodist Protestant Church.

The AUMP church is also responsible for the oldest black church festival in the country, Big August Quarterly, which began in 1814. The church held its meetings once every four months, but it was the August meeting that most followers attended. It was the only time when free blacks and enslaved blacks were allowed to celebrate together. There was much singing and praising. In the forties and fifties, my mother and older siblings remembered when almost all blacks from Delaware still attended.

"We would dress up and parade from downtown over to Mother AUMP, for August Quarterly," my mother said.

It was a proud time. African Americans dressed in their finest clothes and would promenade for everyone to see how beautiful they were. The Quarterly still exists today, but has nowhere near the attendance it had in its heyday.

At the age of twelve, I joined my friend Barbara's church, the Mother Church of God in Christ. It was a Pentecostal church. The Church of God in Christ is the country's largest Pentecostal and African American Christian denomination. COGIC was started in 1907 by Bishop Charles Harrison Mason when he was expelled from the Baptist Church for his radical beliefs of salvation, sanctification, and holiness. Every Sunday we marched in to the church's theme song:

*This is the Church of God in Christ,*
*This is the Church of God in Christ,*
*You can't join in, you've got to be born in,*
*I love the church of God in Christ.*

The church and its leaders taught that the Bible was the only, and infallible, written word of God. We believed in the Holy Spirit and that it was essential for personal salvation. A person had to tarry or pray hard for the Holy Spirit to dwell within them; this was evidenced by that person speaking in tongues, a supernatural language given by God.

In the Church of God in Christ we were not allowed to wear pants, makeup, or jewelry, other than a watch. We could not smoke or drink, dance, or go to the movies, a skating rink, or a bowling alley. Swimming in a bathing suit was not permitted, but you could walk in the water in long skirts just deep enough to get your feet wet. These rules have since changed, and today, as the old folks say, "You can hardly tell a COGIC woman from a Methodist one."

Still, I "loved the Church of God in Christ." Even with all its rules and regulations it was somehow joyful and exuberant. It was my spiritual refuge.

I was there from the time the doors opened until they were closed. During the week, I would go there after I finished my after-school job, so I would be there six days of the week. I prayed and fasted and prayed. I asked God to save my mother and to give her redemption. When I would get home from service, my siblings would hit and tease me for being the "church girl," but the beatings and name-calling did little to deter me. If anything, they made me even more determined to sanctify, or separate, myself from the "world." Their treatment fed my belief that I was being persecuted for Jesus' sake.

The church was where I could take my burdens to the Lord, and, as the song goes, "leave them there." This was in the seventies, when people wore bright African clothing, big jewelry, and Afros. The church was against that kind of "unrighteous" behavior, but our pastor, the Reverend Ross Raincy, told us that God was not concerned with our clothes, but cared about our heart and soul. He taught us that God dwelled within us, that we were to be a light for the world to see so that others might find their way.

Rainey was a radical thinker for his time, and even more radical for the Church of God in Christ. After I got to know him and his wife, Thelma, known as "Na-Nan" to me and "Mother Rainey" to most other members, I was able to ask about their unorthodox approach to COGIC teachings. I found out that Rainey had attended Crozer Theological Seminary in Chester, Pennsylvania, the same divinity school that Dr. Martin Luther King Jr. attended from 1948 until 1951. Crozer's motto was "Education for service is a way of life for Crozer, a forward-thinking seminary." Their brochure boasted that Crozer men and women, students and teachers, discover the reality that religion leads to service.

Students at Crozer were required to think outside of their traditional beliefs and were challenged in their faith. Rainey would also challenge us in our thinking.

"How will people know what you believe if you don't show love?" he would ask. He was unlike the typical COGIC preachers of that time. He was extremely soft-spoken and did not use the loud call-and-response preaching technique. He was known as a teacher of the gospel rather than a preacher. He did not wear the high-fashioned suits of most Pentecostal preachers; instead he wore black suits with white clerics' collars, something rarely worn by black Pentecostal preachers of the day. He encouraged us to study the gospels and to "read up on" history.

"History," he said, "has a lot to teach us. If you don't learn her lessons you'll wish you had."

He taught that everyone was equal in God's eyes and that no one should be turned away from God's love. His liberation theology (a theological belief that demands that the Christian church work for the needs of the poor and fight for economic and political justice) was easy for me to understand. I needed to believe it because it had been a part of my life all along.

These beliefs found their way from the Quakers and John Hunn, from Africa and my great-grandfather John Henry Freeman, to my mother and down to me. Still, I had a hard time fully grasping God's love because of the pain of my circumstances. Even while I attended church and listened to sermons of liberation, I harbored a great deal of anger and resentment about my own poverty and hardships. Soon my anger gave way to insecurity, which manifested in the form of an attitude; the greater the insecurity, the bigger the attitude. It's no wonder that a mad dog bites the hand that feeds him; he's mad.

My family was looked down on, and I did nothing to make people think otherwise. My attitude spilled over into my schoolwork and, consequently, my grades suffered. The one class I could count on for a good grade was chorus. I loved to sing. My sister Chris tells me that I sang before I would talk. If someone asked me a question, I would sing the answer. I sang in the church choir and at school. Eventually, my love for singing got me noticed for something other than a bad attitude, and that's when I started to clean up my act.

The writer Paulo Coelho points out that when a person seeks his purpose in life, the universe conspires to help him achieve it.

Education was something that I longed for. I had secretly yearned to go to college even though no one in my family had ever been. I had no idea of what it would be like, or how to go about getting there. I just knew that once I got there I would be able to learn, and I felt that learning would be my way out of poverty.

I started to get my act together and my music teacher took notice. Leander Morris was one of those teachers whom every child should have. He entered me into every singing contest

that he heard about. One day on the way to one of those con-
tests, Mr. Morris asked me what I wanted to be in life. I told
him that I really liked to read and that one day I would like to
be a writer or a social worker. He said that he understood the
writer part, but wanted to know what made me aspire to social
work.

I told him how the previous summer I had gotten my
first job that was not a cleaning job. It was part of a state-
government-funded program designed to expose poor children to careers rather than the dead-end jobs we normally
took. My first and only choice had been to work with a chemist.
Outside of music, science had been the class that held my attention most. I loved the idea that everything we see could
be dissected to the tiniest level of abstraction; and because
Delaware was the home of the DuPont Chemical Company, my
mind had already been exposed to what science could do. That
summer, my wish came true when I was assigned the job of
chemist's assistant. I was elated. I dreamed about going to
work in a lab coat and goggles and about winning a Nobel Prize
for something. I had no real idea of what I would do, but that's
what the job was for—to expose me to chemistry.

When I showed up for my summer job, I was ready. I had
rebraided my hair in the tiny cornrows that were fashionable
then and had cleaned and pressed my best skirt. I used some
of my cleaning money to get a new white linen top and a new
pair of shoes. I was sharp and ready. My dream was shattered,
however, when I arrived early and was told by the black secre-

tary that I would not do for the position. My braids were not professional, she said, and my linen blouse should have been ironed.

I wanted to scream and tell her that my blouse was linen and was supposed to look the way it did. I wanted to tell her that I had taken longer on my hair than I ever had before and that every cornrow was perfectly straight. I wanted to tell her that she was the secretary and not the chemist I had been sent to work with, but I said none of that. I lowered my head and told her thanks for the advice and went to the job-site office that had given me the assignment in the first place.

People should know how easily they can kill a child's spirit. They should be forced to take a class on the precious and precarious nature of a child's dream. I still wonder how many children who have been dealt a similar fate have ended up in prison or dead because some adult blocked the doorway to their dreams.

The job counselor was angered by what happened and called the secretary to tell her so. The secretary told the counselor to tell me to change my hair and I could come back, but the counselor, who wore an Afro, said no student/worker would be coming to that job site. The counselor was angry with the woman but she tried not to show it. "Why do we treat each other this way?" she angrily mumbled. "And over hair."

She apologized to me for the woman's behavior and said that all the summer jobs had been taken and the only job left was with the food stamp office. I could go there and be a file

clerk and maybe something else would open up. I went to the
food stamp office and was greeted by a white caseworker who
immediately took me around the office to introduce me to the
other employees.

"Look at her hair," she said to everyone there. "She did it
herself, it's just beautiful," she said.

Her appreciation and warmth made me so happy that I took
to the job like I was born for it. Not only would I file the case
folders, but I also started to read them. I would find discrep-
ancies and issues that needed to be handled that the caseworkers had missed. The supervisor was so impressed with my
work, they created a job for me. After a while, I was not just fil-
ing, I was helping to create new files and sorting through
forms, making the caseworkers' job a bit easier. I had a respect for social workers and all that they were faced with.

So when Mr. Morris asked me what I was going to do with
my life, I told him all about my summer job in social work and
my dream to be a writer, and he introduced me to Karen
Denton. Ms. Denton was his friend and an English teacher.
She taught advanced placement English and literature. I had
not been a candidate for any AP classes, but Ms. Denton decided to allow me to give her class a try. She was impressed by
my knowledge of black literature and the classics. Because of
my sister Christine's exposure to the classics on PBS, with
Alistair Cook's Masterpiece Theatre, I had been treated to the
best of both worlds.

Ms. Denton saw my potential and got me involved with

Upward Bound, a government-funded program that was designed to help poor children prepare for college. Once I was ready for college, I had no way to pay, but a wealthy benefactor, Terry Evenson, had just created a scholarship for a student like me at Jacksonville University, where I had applied. Once I got to college, I majored in sociology and worked hard and won honors for academic achievements and leadership. My professors told me that I was graduate school material, so I applied to Kent State and won a scholarship and received a research fellowship.

I was well on my way, and the journey had been made possible by the hands of many. Much like for those before me, success would not be easy, but it was possible. As my mother had said, "The world is full of nasty people, but for every bad one, there's a good one waiting to help."

Graduate school was not easy. It was challenging at every level. There was very little support coming from family or my church friends. When I applied to college, they all wondered why. In their minds, I had already been offered a permanent job at the food stamp office, and if that didn't work, I had my cleaning jobs. People wondered why I would leave paying jobs to go to a school that didn't pay anything. I know now that if you have not tasted a better way of thinking and living, you learn to like what you have and dislike what you don't have.

I had no financial support from family and hardly any emotional support from my friends, but something inside of me urged me onward and I kept moving. Once I had found a way out of poverty through education, I would not turn back.

My graduate school adviser was Dr. Elizabeth Mullins. She was as tough as she was brilliant.

Dr. Mullins, a white woman, was conducting research on elite black women. She wanted to know the factors that led to their success. She had hypothesized that elite black women (those who had obtained a specified level of financial success) had several things going for them that their cultural counterparts did not. One factor was years of freedom. Dr. Mullins believed that women who descended from families who were free before the emancipation of 1865 had a head start on other black families. Prior to working with her, I had not given any thought to the fact that in the United States, freedom from slavery did not happen for all blacks at the same time. African Americans are the descendants of slaves, but not all slaves were "set free" at the same time.

There were several ways a person of bondage came to freedom. Some were given letters of manumission, which provided legal freedom. This often happened when a slave owner died and stipulated in his will that certain enslaved blacks be set free. In many cases, these enslaved blacks were also offspring of the slave owner.

Freedom also occurred in northern states before it did in the South. But it didn't happen at one time and rarely did slavery end when it officially ended. In other words, most free states had an official end date (when it ended on paper) and an actual date of its cessation (when slaves were finally set free). In Vermont, slavery officially ended in 1777 and actually ended the same year, while in Pennsylvania, the official date was 1780 but the actual date when there was no slave trafficking, ownership of persons, or use thereof did not occur until 1845. Massachusetts, New Hampshire, Connecticut, Rhode Island, and New York had officially ended slavery as early as 1799, but the actual end dates for these states were as late as 1848. New Jersey officially ended slavery in 1804 but did not release all enslaved blacks until 1865. At the time of the Civil War, Alabama, Arkansas, Delaware, Florida, Georgia, Kentucky, Louisiana, Maryland, Mississippi, North Carolina, South Carolina, Tennessee, Texas, Virginia (which included West Virginia), the District of Columbia, and the Nebraska Territory were all slave states. By the end of slavery, Delaware was the northernmost slave state. In the northern part of the state, by 1840 most blacks were free, with only 13 percent enslaved. I can only imagine what it must have been like to know that freedom was a short distance away.

Another form of liberation occurred when enslaved blacks bought, fought, and claimed their own freedom. There are actual cases in which enslaved blacks sued for their freedom, as occurred with the Africans aboard the *Amistad*. Before the enactment of the Fugitive Slave Law, blacks who got to free states had the right to be free. Enslaved blacks often received assistance from the free blacks of those states. An enslaved person would be asked, "Do you wish to be free?" If the individual said yes, the free black would provide shelter and assistance toward a free life.

William Still recorded the case of John Henry Pettifoot, who had been hired out to McHenry and McCullough, "tobacconists" of Petersburg, Virginia, whom Pettifoot found "more oppressive than he agreed for." John decided that he "shouldn't have to work so hard for nothing." The woman who had "leased" him to McHenry and McCullough had told John that he would be set free when she died. John decided that he should not have to wait, so, as he said, he "picked up his bed and walked." John escaped to Philadelphia as a stowaway on a steam liner.

When Dr. Mullins pointed out that the greater rates of ancestral freedom played a role in the status of elite women, I was forced to look at the idea of freedom differently. Prior to then, I believed that slavery ended for all blacks at the same time, the signing of the Emancipation Proclamation. When I asked her about this variable in her research she grunted and said, "Think about it, Bert; do you believe that white people are smarter than blacks?" I told her that I didn't. My exposure to whites in undergraduate school had destroyed any thought that I might have had regarding the intellectual superiority of whites.

"Do you think that whites work harder or deserve more?" she then asked.

"Of course not," I replied.

"Well, think about it. The only advantage white folks have

over blacks is that they had free labor on stolen land and they were free to do what they wanted."

I immediately saw her rationale. Mullins believed that black women who were extremely successful probably came from families that had a "head start" on the masses. Her research findings supported the hypothesis that women who were much more successful than their peers came from families that had been free before emancipation.

Another important variable for the success of the black woman was the level of education that her mother had. One of the giants in American history is anthropologist, author, and voodoo priestess Zora Neale Hurston, whose mother was said to be the "prettiest and smartest woman in Eatonville, Florida."

"When a mother is exposed to a structured way of thinking, the child will desire more," Mullins once barked.

I soon found out that Dr. Mullins's bark was much worse than her bite. She was tough; she yelled at all of her graduate students and would constantly point out just how ignorant we all were. Ignorance was not a horrible thing for Dr. Mullins. It just meant that we did not know.

"You're just ignorant, Bert," she said. "That's okay, we can fix ignorant, but there's nothing I can do for stupid," she said.

Dr. Mullins would scream and yell at the slightest error. She would send the brightest students home crying and begging for a reassignment. I had been raised in a house full of screamers, so Dr. Mullins was almost normal to me.

One day I was trying to run a statistical analysis on some of her data. I had been instructed to calculate the mean level of education for the mother of the women in the sample. I began to perform the somewhat simple task, but soon realized that I had a problem. Under Dr. Mullins's tutelage, I learned that all data told a story and that it was up to the researcher to interpret the story the statistics told. This data was telling me that the elite black women in the sample did not have mothers who had more than an average amount of education; instead it told me that most of their mothers had no education at all. I knew that this could not be true. The women in the study were black doctors and lawyers. They were older than me by at least twenty years. I knew that women from that time period had to get their inspiration from somewhere. I decided to look at the actual questionnaires that the data had come from, which would be a daunting task, since the study included hundreds of women. I had been looking at the handwritten questionnaires closely for more than a week when Dr. Mullins stormed into the research lab.

"What's taking you so damned long?" she barked.

I tried to give her a short answer. I had learned from my mother that hard women did not have time for long, drawn-out responses; they liked the truth, plain, simple, and quick.

"The data doesn't fit" was all I could manage. If looks could kill, you wouldn't be reading this.

"What do you mean it doesn't fit? Are you stupid?"

I decided to give her the long answer; I started from the beginning and told her how I had discovered a discrepancy and hadn't wanted to tell her until I was certain.

"I think the data has been miscoded," I told her. She asked me to explain exactly what I meant. I told her that I could see that in instances where a respondent did not know her mother's level of education, the previous graduate assistant had coded the response as a zero instead of a nine. The number nine represented no answer, while the number zero meant no education.

Dr. Mullins looked at me for a long time, scratched her head, and said, "I can see that you are not the typical dumb graduate assistant. I need to give you the whole picture, not just your task."

She walked toward the door, turned, and said, "Good job, Bert."

From then on, our relationship changed. She was the mentor I needed. Later on she would explain to me that most people wanted to know just enough to get by.

"Discipline your mind to yearn for the whole picture, Bert, and you will always be successful," Dr. Mullins said.

When her research project was completed, she was able to prove that education was the key factor to the success of black women and that longer periods of freedom in the family's background also played an important part.

My mother was a very wise woman. She was also incredibly bright, but when she went to live with her mother, Caroline, she was forced to drop out of school. But she always loved reading and learning. I know now that my love for education comes from her; back when I was a child, though, I felt that my mother and I had very little in common.

Dr. Mullins passed away before I could finish my dissertation, but before she did she told me to study things that were close to my heart, and that when I did, the truth would lead the way.

Just as it took many people to aid, assist, care for, and educate enslaved people out of bondage, it took many to help me find my way out of poverty up toward liberation, where you control your own movements and what you think and produce.

*Part Two*

# Race

A fully functional multiracial society cannot be achieved without
a sense of history and open, honest dialogue.
—CORNEL WEST

FOUR

# Songs of Freedom

I looked over Jordan and what did I see? A band of angels
coming after me, coming for to carry me home.

—"SWING LOW, SWEET CHARIOT," NEGRO SPIRITUAL

I've always been silently envious of my white peers who can
trace their families back to the great-grandparents of their
great-grandparents. The documentation of white ancestry far
outweighs that of our black counterparts. I am moved by the
works of Alex Haley, Henry Louis Gates, and Lerone Bennett,
whose lives have been dedicated to making the connection to
our historical roots. Still, the lack of genealogical documentation, cultural memory, and interest has created a void in the

ancestral archives of African Americans. There is an old proverb that says, "Those who are in power write the history, while those who suffer write the songs." This is true. African Americans are the ancestors of American music and folktales.

In the moans, the groans, and the shouts of our ancestors lies the story of our struggle and of our progress.

*Oh Freedom*
*Oh Freedom*
*Oh Freedom over me!*
*And before I'd be a slave*
*I'll be buried in my grave*
*And go home to my Lord and be free*
*No more moaning*
*No more moaning*
*No more moaning over me!*
*And before I'd be a slave*
*I'll be buried in my grave*
*And go home to my Lord and be free.*

The people who sang these songs of freedom had been enslaved or were descendants of people who had been. It becomes all too apparent that freedom for them was not just about physical freedom. For those enslaved ancestors, freedom was also a state of mind, one that enabled them to recognize that even while they were in shackles their minds were free.

When we look closely at the Negro spirituals that originated before the abolition of slavery, an interesting pattern emerges; songs like "Swing Low, Sweet Chariot" and "Gospel Train" contain codes. In them are the encoded instructions for the passage to freedom.

*Get on board, lil' children*
*Get on board, lil' children*
*Get on board, lil' children*
*There's room for many more*

This was not a happy song about heaven; it was an encoded message that the freedom train, or Underground Railroad, was coming through. The train was coming, but you had to meet it at the station; in other words, you had to come out and meet your freedom.

Among abolitionist historians, there is a great deal of discussion regarding the amount of attention given to white abolitionists versus black abolitionists. When information about abolitionists has reached mass media in films like *Amistad* and *Amazing Grace*, the story is often met with criticism of having been "too white" and not "black enough." Meanwhile, the masses that were previously unaware of these stories in the first place choose sides based on their race rather than their need for more information. Never ones to be too creative or to step too far out of the box, Hollywood executives respond to the hype by playing it safe, failing even to look in the direction of the white-folks-working-with-the-black-folks during-slavery stories ever again.

The Underground Railroad was not a physical railroad. In some places, there were actual underground caves and caverns where fugitives or runaways were hidden; however, the Underground Railroad was the name given to the interconnected workings of individuals and groups who believed in and worked for the abolition of slavery. The term "Underground Railroad" is believed to have originated from the belief that a runaway black must have somehow gone underground, since his whereabouts were unknown. The Underground Railroad itself was a very organized and sophisticated movement of "fugitives of slavery," as they came to be known from slave plantations up to freedom. Individuals, black and white, slave and free, would help the fugitives in their escape. While there are many amazing tales of escape that range from mailing oneself to freedom in a box (Henry "Box" Brown, 1849) to a husband and wife escaping with one passing for white while the other acted as a slave (William and Ellen Craft, 1848), it should be recognized that most runaways did just that; they ran and walked and sailed to their freedom. Along the way, the fugitives met up with people who came to be known as "stationmasters" and "conductors" of the Underground Railroad. These people provided shelter, food, clothing, directions, and the inspiration to move on. It should also be noted that the assistance of a white conductor also provided the "fugitive" with evidence of the fact that not all whites were slaveholders.

Slave owners did their best to indoctrinate enslaved blacks with the idea that slavery was a natural, God-ordained institution and that it was the right and privilege of all whites to own and control the lives of black people. These slave owners did their jobs "well." They used forms of torture, religious indoctrination, and the art of pitting black against black in their efforts to maintain control. Enslaved blacks were taught to believe that no one would ever help them run away and that life outside the plantation was worse than anything they endured on the plantation. Because laws prohibited slaves from reading and they were punished or put to death for trying to do so, they had little idea that some whites were writing and teaching against the bonds of slavery. Antislavery literature was also illegal in the South, thereby preventing the ideas of abolitionists from spreading among proslavery white folks.

Without having access to written materials or even the talk of freedom, enslaved blacks used songs and chants to get the word out that the Freedom Train was coming through. Fugitives knew that the "chariot was waiting" meant an escort was nearby. "A band of angels coming after me" was not a reference to angelic escorts to heaven, but to human freedom fighters literally coming over a hilltop (over "Jordan") to meet runaways at the "station" (or designated location of meeting).

America has not spent enough time looking closely at the abolitionist movement. It's no wonder we know nothing about the magnitude and numbers of those who fought to end slavery. I am amazed when I have to explain to people that John Brown was a white man who led a band of white rebels in a

bloody revolt against slavery. People are astonished when I re-
cite the tale of Nat Turner, the black preacher who led one of
the deadliest battles for freedom. Even when people think they
know the story of Nat Turner, they are astonished to learn that
he escaped to freedom, but after hearing the voice of the Lord
speak to his heart he returned. Turner believed that when God
told him to "seek ye first the kingdom of God and all his righteousness, and your desires will be added unto you"(Matthew
6:33), He was telling him to go back into slavery, gather an
army, and then He would grant him his freedom.

"Why would Nat go back into slavery?" my listeners often
ask. I can only tell them what I have read, that Nat Turner believed his real mission was not just his own freedom but the
actual destruction of slavery itself.

While the stories of John Brown, Nat Turner, and even
Harriet Tubman are somewhat well known, the details of these
amazing lives are known only in certain historians' circles.
Rarely if ever are such stories told around dinner tables and at
family gatherings. We African Americans have no seder meals
or Passover celebrations where the tale of our Exodus from
bondage is retold. It's no wonder that we know little or nothing about the rebels who served as conductors and stationmasters who led the train to freedom. Some stories are out
there in old dusty history books and Civil War documents.
Many were written by the conductors and riders themselves,
while others were written years later in an attempt to remind
us of the struggle. Too often, though, the tales are drowned out

by the noise of the debate over who should tell it and what should be included.

When we look closely at the abolitionist movement, we come to see that it was in fact a movement. The Civil Rights Movement of the 1960s had its heroes and leaders who stood out from others, and it also had a multitude of people behind it. So did the abolitionist movement. When I rejected my mother's story about abolitionist John Hunn, I refused to see my own family's connection to it. When I opened my eyes to John Hunn, I opened my eyes to myself.

FIVE

# My Native Land

A Slave is one who is in the power of a master to whom he belongs.
The master may sell him, dispose of his person, his industry,
his labor, he can do nothing, possess nothing, nor acquire
any things but which must belong to his master.

—LOUISIANA SLAVE CODE ARTICLE 3

Knowledge is power and love is a weapon. Armed with both, I was prepared to battle my ignorance. I would use my mother's stories as a starting point.

When I found John Hunn, I found myself.

Like the full story of black folks during slavery, John Hunn's life and deeds were hidden in scholarly text; they were in bits and pieces locked behind the glass walls of archival information in our nation's libraries.

In my initial computer search for John Hunn, I was rewarded with blurbs and lines that described him as the southernmost conductor of the Underground Railroad. I found short passages that described him as a Quaker and an abolitionist, but little else.

Still, my heart really did leap with joy. I had heard his name many times, but to actually see it in print gave credence to what I had only now come to believe. But my joy was short-lived when embarrassment crept in. I was embarrassed by my ignorance to the real fact; I was ashamed of the prejudice that allowed me to reject the idea of a decent white person during slavery. Most important, I was ashamed that I had written off my own mother's stories.

There was never a reason to doubt her. She had not lied to me in the past. She never made promises.

"Promises are made to be broken," she would say. "Ain't no need to make them if you are just going to break them. If I say it's so, then it is. If I don't, it ain't."

But I had rejected her stories because I thought what I knew was right.

As I searched through the existing files and documents, I was forced to see how wrong I was. Each piece of evidence gave way to new questions.

As a sociologist, I am drawn to ask why. I needed to know what had set John Hunn apart from others during slavery, what convicted his heart to do the right thing. I would soon see that John Hunn was not alone in his actions, and I would have to rethink my query. The question, What set John Hunn apart from white men during slavery?, would become, Why didn't I know about the magnitude of the abolitionist movement? Why had I not seen the many forms it took and the diversity of its participants?

There is an old saying in the black community that "if you want to hide the truth, put it in a book." I quickly learned that there was no search engine or Wikipedialike source that could paint the picture of what I needed to know. I had to go on a search that would sometimes leave me excited and at other moments angry.

In between my mother's hospital stays and my trips lecturing for large associations and corporate groups, I took trips to Delaware to the public and university libraries.

I began to collect and read rare and hard-to-find books about slavery and abolition. Soon I was purchasing original documents that left signs and markers of the struggles from slavery to freedom. From there, I've been able to piece together the story of my family and the folks who helped along the way. I can see how history repeats itself and how, as I wrote in *Redemption Song* in 2000, "we had traded in one form of slavery for another when we turned our backs on God, wisdom and on love." Exploring my family's history and that of John Hunn has made me understand the ties that bind. I can agree with the Apostle Paul when he said in Romans 8:28 that "all things work together for the good of those who love God and are called according to God's purpose." Getting the call is easy; it's the listening and responding that demand the work.

We are connected to the past of our forefathers and

foremothers by more than DNA. Their memories run through our blood. We are the embodiment of their unfulfilled longings and are charged with the task of fulfilling their dreams. Choreographer Alvin Ailey often spoke of blood memories as deep-rooted impulses that have been transmitted from one generation to the next. He believed that unspoken memories of black folks can be retrieved through the dance, music, and stories of African Americans.

The memories of my ancestors were calling to me. They demanded that I listen. I was, after all, a storyteller. But before I could tell the stories of other black folks, I had to get my own right.

Moments of awareness happen in a flash. In that single instant in time, we are given a choice: choose truth or go on as we are.

We have a saying in my home state: "Delaware was the first state to have slaves and the last to let them go." Most people don't think of Delaware as a slave state and they certainly don't think of it as southern. It borders Maryland to the south and Pennsylvania to the north. For many runaway slaves, Delaware was literally the gap between slavery and freedom.

Delaware is known as the state that started a nation and is called the first state; its representatives were the first of the original thirteen to ratify the constitution. Before Europeans came to her shores, Delaware was home to Unami Lenape, or Delaware Indians, as they later came to be called. These Native Americans were proficient in cultivating farming techniques that were previously unknown to the Europeans who would settle there later. Delaware was also home to the Nanticoke, the Minqua, and the Iroquois.

In 1631, the Dutch were the first Europeans to settle in Delaware when they established a trading post, but within a year, all of the settlers were killed in a trade dispute with Delaware's original natives. In 1638, a Swedish colony was established, then in 1655 the Dutch regained control and took over the entire colony, adding it to the Dutch New Netherlands, which included parts of what is now New York, New Jersey, Pennsylvania, Connecticut, and Rhode Island. The first black slave, known in history books only as "Black Anthony," came to Delaware with the Swedes in 1636, but it was the Dutch West Indian Trading Company that made slavery a main part of Delaware's history.

New York and Delaware were the first states to import "slaves" from Africa into the New World. It was apparent to the Dutch and other settlers early on that Native Americans would not be forced to do their labor. The natives were too familiar with the territory and outnumbered the European settlers. In contrast, Africans were a long way from home. They did not speak the language of their captors, they spoke many different languages among themselves, and the whites did not bother to learn any African language. Many of the Africans brought to Delaware's shores arrived in chains from the Ivory Coast, Gambia, Angola, and Guinea.

The transformation from African to African American began within the hulls of the slave ships, where people were crammed and shackled together like animals. Without having a common language, the enslaved Africans learned to communicate with one another in songs and sounds. This new language would be necessary when they were delivered in chains along the eastern seaboard.

Initially plantations were vast; many hands were needed to plant and harvest the fields of wheat, corn, and tobacco. When Europeans gave up the ways of their motherland, inheritance laws shifted from the practice of bequeathing property to the eldest son to the more "democratic" transfer to all surviving children. Consequently, plantations were divided up and became smaller. Paying little attention to the ways of the Native Americans, who rotated crops and hunted for what they needed rather than all they could sell, the land was overworked and wild animals became less plentiful. If life doesn't teach you a lesson, Mother Nature will; she did so for the colonialist settlers who refused to listen. After yielding all the crops she could, the fields became more and more difficult to harvest, causing farmers to find other sources of income. Corn and wheat replaced tobacco and fishing, and textiles supplemented the loss of income that had transferred to the Deep South.

With smaller plantations, Delaware took on the interesting distinction of being a slave state in what we think of as the North. Even more interesting is the fact that during the Civil War, when more than six hundred thousand people were killed in the battle between North and South, Delaware, the southern slave state, never seceded from the Union. Even though the export of slavery was abolished in 1789, and the Emancipation Proclamation was signed in 1863, it would be many years later, in 1900, that the Fourteenth Amendment ("All persons born or naturalized in the United States, and subject to the jurisdiction thereof, are citizens of the United States and of the State wherein they reside. No State shall make or enforce any law which shall abridge the privileges or immunities of citizens of the United States; nor shall any State deprive any person of life, liberty, or property, without due process of law; nor deny to any person within its jurisdiction the equal protection of the laws") would be ratified by Delaware, the state that started a nation.

Indeed, Delaware has a fascinating history. It is also the home of my American ancestors.

# SIX

# *Setting the Captives Free*

"Come to the edge," he said.
They said: "We are afraid."
"Come to the edge," he said.
They came.
He pushed them, and they flew.

—APOLLINAIRE

John Hunn is as much a part of my heritage as my great-granddaddy John Henry Freeman, the sharecropper and overseer on John Hunn's farm. Before I can tell you about my great-granddaddy, I have to tell you about John Hunn, the man whose name I tried to tarnish in my novel *Redemption Song*.

John Hunn was called to the ministry in a rather ordinary way. There were no trumpets blaring; he didn't fall off his horse and go blind; he simply and quietly saw the need, as he stated in his courtroom trial, to "set liberty to them that are bruised."

John Hunn was born to comfortable wealth in Delaware on June 25, 1818. The Hunn family owned and operated a large mill and foundry. They leased farmland and owned a farming establishment and sailing vessels. Although John was born to privilege, he would suffer early the tragedies of death. His mother, Harriet J. Alston, died after the birth of his sister in 1819 when John was just a year old. His grandfather died a year later, and then in 1821, his father, Ezekiel, passed away. John, his younger sister, and an older brother were left in the care of his aunt and then went to live with an older half-sister, Patience, who would later become instrumental in his spiritual conversion.

John's father was said to have been a great abolitionist who had assisted "many poor from the house of bondage." Surely John grew up hearing stories about his father's life and work, but the loss of family must also have played an important role in his decision to help keep families together.

Delaware's state motto, "Liberty and Independence," is incorporated into her state flag. Many of the settlers came to her shore in search of the privilege of land ownership and the opportunities that were denied in their native homes. White Delawareans knew the importance of freedom, yet they felt secure in the right to hold captive the freedom of their darker brothers and sisters. By 1770 slaves made up 20 to 25 percent of the total population, and more than 95 percent of blacks were enslaved. But by the 1840s, a period that became significant for John Hunn and my family, slaves were only 3 percent of the state's population, with only 13 percent of all blacks enslaved.

Slavery in Delaware was harsh. It was not a cotton state, and because few Delawareans owned the large year-round plantations that the South became wealthy from, enslaved blacks were "rented," or indentured, from one plantation to the next. They could be indentured for six years to one person and then for six years to someone else. No part of slavery was good for anyone involved. In his book *A View of the American Slavery Question* (1836), Elijah Porter Barrows pointed out that the slave system "degrades the entire colored population of the United States." Barrows felt that slaves were not the only ones to suffer under the hands of slavery.

> *In the free states too, the free negro is doomed to feel the oppressive influence of the unrighteous system. For he belongs to the race enslaved, despised, and trampled under foot for two centuries; with whom the community have always been accustomed to associate the ideas of servitude, infirmity and degradation.*

Because of the 1787 ban on the exportation of slaves in Delaware, slave owning was less profitable than it was in more southern states, where the profiting from the sale and purchase of slaves helped plantation owners become wealthy. With fewer slaves to work, the ones who lived in Delaware were worked hard and shuffled around from place to place with very little familial contacts or connections. Additionally, a "cleansing" of the culture occurred as blacks were less connected to the cultural traditions of their African heritage. I don't want to be accused of arguing that Delaware blacks had it harder than others during slavery, but it must be noted that the conditions of weather, and the small numbers of enslaved blacks and treatment thereof, made for unique and difficult conditions for those in bondage there. With freedom only a few days' walk away, the proximity to Pennsylvania must have made the longing for freedom even more painful. The abolition of slavery in Pennsylvania was signed into law in 1847, but the institution of slavery had already weakened by then. Fewer and fewer Pennsylvanian farmers owned slaves or believed that anyone should.

John Hunn was born to a family that believed all beings should be free and in God's eyes were created equal. John Hunn was born to Quaker parents at a time when Quakers were finding out firsthand that the religious freedom that our country was established upon did not extend itself to all religions, races, and creeds.

The Society of Friends was formed in the mid-1600s in England by George Fox. Fox did not set out to establish a new religion, but wanted to bring the church back to what he believed it had been during the days of the apostles. He proclaimed the teaching of Peter that Jesus had risen from the dead and now was present in the hearts of his followers in spirit and principles, and was empowering them to live righteously and to do great works. Fox called for a spirit-filled Christianity that was egalitarian and inclusive of all, regardless of race, sex, or class.

In 2008, churches are still segregated by race and class. There is a saying in the black community that "11 a.m. on a Sunday is the most segregated hour in American life." In most denominations, women are still regarded as second-class citizens. It should be easy to imagine how foreign Fox's ideas were in the 1600s.

The Society of Friends came to be known as Quakers when George Fox and his followers were brought before a judge in the court of England for refusing to pay tithes, take oaths in court, or remove their hats in the presence of kings and others in power. When Fox informed the judge that even he should tremble at the Word of the Lord, the judge called Fox a "quaker." The term took and, though it was meant to offend, it was worn proudly.

Quakers came to the United States for the same reason others had, to flee religious persecution, but they soon learned that their ideas of freedom and equality were no more accepted in the colonies than they had been in England.

Quakers were hardworking and honest people. In fact, they came to be the very symbol of honesty and good values. The image of a Quaker became the trademark of Quaker Oats when in 1901 the founders of the company felt that the image of a Quaker would immediately inform the customers that the cereal was a good value made by honest hands.

Although this was the general view, the Society of Friends was also looked upon by some as a group of troublemakers. Its religious ideas about equality helped fuel and fan the flames of abolition in this country. As early as 1688, the Society of Friends was the first white group to denounce slavery as unacceptable in the eyes of God, stating, "There is a liberty of conscience which is right and reasonable, and there ought to be likewise liberty of the body."

Still, there were Quakers who were slaveholders. Most notable is William Penn, the founder of Pennsylvania Colony, who in 1701 freed his slaves and became a part of the abolitionist movement.

John Hunn was born into a Quaker family, but his parents died in his youth, then in the mid-1830s he was disowned by the Cherry Street meeting (or church group) in Philadelphia when he married a non-Quaker. To young John this abandonment had to be another major trial for the orphan and another factor in his high regard for family and community.

John and his wife, Mary Allen Swallow, were allowed back into the fold in 1848 when John officially apologized for "marrying out of a union." His apology was accepted and his membership transferred to the Camden, Delaware, meeting.

John, who was educated at the Quaker Academy in Bordertown, New Jersey, had inherited wealth from the large estates

left by his father and grandfather, and was trained by and con-
ducted business with other prominent families. He became a
successful farmer and textile merchant, but in 1845, when
John was visiting his sister Patience, a devout evangelist in the
Quaker faith, she took one look at his expensive cloak and told
him to "take off his Babylonish garment, for I am led to believe
that if thee is faithful, thee would also be a preacher."

I cannot begin to imagine what went through the mind of
the twenty-seven-year-old John. By then he and Mary had had
the first of their four children. He was a successful family man
and well established in his community, and now he was being
called to the ministry.

Complete spiritual transformations are as wonderful as
they are rare. When a person turns his life around, he creates
opportunities for others to do the same. Surely Patience had
no idea of the impact that her younger brother would have on
the history of this country; she would never have dreamed of
the real and personal impact he would have on my life.

The next time Patience saw her brother, he was wearing the
simple suit that would clothe him for most of the remainder of
his life. The suit had been made from the expensive cloak; now
it was worn over a heart that had been transformed.

# SEVEN

# Set the Captives Free

For the better security of the peace and friendship now centered
into by the contracting parties, against all infractions of the same,
by the citizens of either party, to the prejudice of others, neither
mutual liking. And it is further argued between parties aforesaid,
that neither shall entertain, or give countenance to, the enemies of
the other, or protect, in their respective states, criminal fugitives,
servants, or slaves, but the same to apprehend and secure,
and deliver to the state or states, to which such enemies,
criminals, servants or slaves, respectively belong . . .

—FUGITIVE SLAVE LAW OF 1793, ARTICLE 4

John Hunn took his calling to the ministry quite literally. Like
most Quakers of the time, he viewed slavery as an unholy act
of oppression, a sinful institution by its very nature. Quakers
not only believed that all beings were equal, they also es-

poused that each individual carried within him the light of God and that if we were to diminish the light of another, we would dampen the spark we needed. The beliefs of Quakers played a very important role in the abolition of slavery. They were the first whites to denounce slavery in Europe and the United States.

While the abolition of slavery was discussed by Quakers in 1688, it was not until 1696 that the Quaker Society officially declared that it was against slavery. Still, there was a division within the Society in regard to slavery. It was not until 1780, when Quakers finally passed the Act for the Gradual Abolishment of Slavery, that they came to be known throughout the world for their fight against slavery. Among them were Anthony Benzet, who influenced well-known abolitionists like Benjamin Rush and Benjamin Franklin. They worked along with the Pennsylvania Society, which was the basis of operation for the great abolitionists Lucretia Mott, Susan B. Anthony, and William Still. Other religious denominations later joined the Quakers in their movement for the abolition of slavery. Free black denominations that had always fought to end slavery were the first religious groups to join ranks with the Quakers, and later Presbyterians, Methodists, and certain divisions of the Baptist faith joined in the fight. Most Christians who opposed slavery did so from the belief that slavery was a sin, an abomination in the eyes of God; however, this belief did not necessarily lead them to believe that blacks were equal to whites. Quakers, on the other hand, saw all men and women as equal. They did not believe that any one group was closer to or more special than another and felt that something as sacred as communion could be experienced by sharing a meal with someone. The "radical" Christianity of the Quakers made it a moral obligation for them to work toward the abolition of slavery. Some wrote pamphlets, while others preached in the streets and meeting houses. Tens of thousands actually joined the Anti-Slavery Reform Society as a result of the Quakers' teachings. Their influence upon the attitude of the nation was so great, many, like John Hunn, were willing to stand at the doorway of oppression and its captors to risk life and limb in the abolition of slavery.

John Hunn and his family gave assistance to hundreds of runaways, or fugitives, as they were known on the Underground Railroad to freedom. He not only preached about the evils of slavery, but risked his reputation and life to help those he called "the downtrodden."

In his book *The Underground Railroad*, written in 1872, William Still cataloged the accounts of fugitives from slavery who made their way up to the Pennsylvania Vigilance Committee. He cites John Hunn as an important and very active conductor who guided many, including Harriet Tubman, up from the lower part of Delaware to northern Wilmington, where Thomas Garrett would assist them on to Philadelphia: "Almost within the lions den, in daily sight of the enemy, in the little slave holding state of Delaware, lived and labored the freedom-loving, earnest, avid, whole-souled Quaker abolitionist, John Hunn."

According to Still, this was dangerous work. When the Fugitive Slave Act of 1793 made it illegal to give aid, assistance, or care to a runaway slave, it created an avenue for vigilante traders, or man-hunters, to make a living by capturing and returning those fugitives.

William Still's book outlines numerous accounts of fines, torture, and deaths of whites and free blacks who sought to help others to freedom. The maintenance of the slave system was serious business; so serious that if an individual in a slave state had won his freedom, he was required to leave that state immediately or risk being sold back into slavery.

The southern part of Delaware was a hotbed of activity for slave trackers. They knew that once a slave made it to the northern part of the state, then on to the Pennsylvania Committee, capture was much more difficult since officers of the law and public officials sometimes looked the other way where issues of slavery were concerned. Many would use the law against the traders, citing lack of evidence as a reason, rather than turn a person over to the slave catchers.

Even in the face of danger, John Hunn and the other members of his family continued their work.

When I first read of the accounts of Hunn and other abolitionists, I was moved and amazed by their heroism. My amazement gave way to frustration, and frustration to sorrow. I was saddened by the fact that none of this history had been made a part of my education.

Healing begins with gratitude. In order for me to be healed from the lasting impact of oppression through slavery, I needed to give thanks for the work that had been done.

My heart could not contain the emotions that came from the understanding that slavery did not go unchallenged. The very fact that there were laws against the education, assistance, and care for those in bondage meant that there was a reason to need them. My mother used to say that "The law is for the lawless." The fugitive laws and slave codes existed for those rebels whose names we hardly even know and rarely ever celebrate.

John Hunn was one of those rebels. He put the welfare of his family on the line many times, but in 1845, when he gave assistance to a band of thirteen runaways and Samuel Burris, a free black man, he and the others were caught and punished for it. The following is an excerpt of John Hunn's personal account to William Still, from *The Underground Railroad*.

*I was washing my hands at the yard pump of my residence near Middleton, New Castle County, Delaware, I looked down the lane and saw a covered wagon slowly approaching my house. The sun had risen and was shining brightly (after a stormy night) on the snow which covered the ground to the depth of six inches . . .*

Hunn goes on to tell how he noticed several men walking alongside the wagon. When the wagon and the men reached his house, one of them, a black man, Samuel Burris, handed him a letter addressed to him or two other abolitionists. The letter was from his cousin Ezekiel Jenkins and informed him that the travelers, a man and his wife, six children, and four "fine looking colored men" were fugitives from slavery. This was the first time Hunn and Burris had met; it would not be the last.

> *The wanderers were gladly welcomed, and made as comfortable as possible until breakfast was ready for them . . . The increase of thirteen in the family was a little embarrassing, but after breakfast they all retired to the barn to sleep on the hay, except the woman and four children who remained in the house.*

The care that was given to the "fugitives" is rather touching. The fact that Hunn expresses embarrassment lends credence to his belief that all people are equal.

Hunn goes on to tell how late that afternoon a neighbor came to spy on his household. The neighbor reported the activities to the constable, who came to arrest the travelers. When the constable asked Hunn if the runaways were in the house, Hunn told him they were not. As they were talking, the man, his wife, and their six children ran into the woods. One of the man-hunters, as they were often called, chased them into the woods. This was late December; the weather was cold and there was snow on the ground. For a northern state, Delaware's climate is somewhat moderate. Still, it can be cold, with temperatures dropping to the single digits and ocean winds bringing snow and freezing rain. The group had already traveled twenty-seven miles to get to Hunn and were exhausted. One of the runaways came back near the house with a butcher's knife in his hand. He would not be taken without a fight. The constable had a gun and threatened to use it. He told Hunn to get the knife away from the "fugitive." Hunn said he would do so only if the constable handed him his gun. Amazingly, the constable did what Hunn asked and the man turned over the knife. The "fugitive" also handed over his pass, certifying that he was free. His name was Samuel Hawkins.

One of the constable's assistants, a man named William Hardcastle, spoke up, saying that he also knew the man to be free; the woman and children, however, were not. He said that the two oldest boys "belonged" to his neighbor.

The group was then taken before the magistrate and John Hunn went along. Fortunately for them, the magistrate, William Street, was a friend of Hunn's. When they arrived, William Hardcastle "lovingly" put his arm around Samuel Hawkins and led him into another room. While there, Hardcastle told Hawkins that if he would give up the two boys, then he, his wife, and their four children would be released to the sheriff. Hunn told Hawkins that he did not think Hardcastle would keep his word, but Hawkins believed he would. The deal was put in writing. When the sheriff arrived, he listened to the group's story but said he did not think the written deal was legal and therefore could not hold the runaways lawfully. The constable offered to get another "commitment" that would be binding and said that the group should be held until he could return.

While they were in jail waiting for the new contract, the sheriff's daughter heard the conversation and sent word to the famed abolitionist Thomas Garrett. Garrett went to the jail with attorney John Wales, who obtained a writ of habeas corpus from Judge Booth. The party was brought before the judge, who discharged them at once. He decided that since there was not enough evidence to hold them, the presumption should be made in favor of freedom.

When I first read this passage in William Still's book, and every time since, I was deeply moved by the acts of everyone involved, but the idea that the judge would choose to err on the side of freedom gives me what Democratic presidential candidate Barack Obama calls "the audacity of hope." By looking closely at this series of events that took place in 1845, I am encouraged to believe, in 2008, that there are still those who are willing to do the right thing, even when the laws of the land are against them. When I read this account, I knew beyond a shadow of a doubt that there will always be a voice of hope that will speak out for justice in the land.

The family was now free. They traveled to Wilmington and then from there to Byberry, Pennsylvania, where they later settled. By the time John Hunn wrote his account of those events to William Still in 1871, Samuel Hawkins and his wife had passed away, but their descendants, who went by the name Hackett, still lived in that area.

Samuel Burris, the free black man who had accompanied the Hawkins family, continued to assist runaways and brought hundreds to the Hunn farm for food, clothing, and shelter, but later was captured and tried himself. He was found guilty and was to be sold back into slavery to serve a term of seven years. According to William Still, "John Hunn and Thomas Garrett were as faithful to him as brothers." They solicited the help of the Philadelphia Anti-Slavery Society, who promptly raised the funds to purchase Burris's freedom.

John Hunn and Thomas Garrett were well-known abolitionists. In fact, Hunn's actions were reported in Maryland's newspapers, which also included the location of his home and made a plea for his neighbors to force him from the place. Hunn welcomed the news of the article. "It enabled many a poor fugitive escaping from the house of bondage to find a hearty welcome," he wrote.

Because he and Garrett were too well-known around the area, Isaac Flint, an abolitionist from Delaware, was chosen to "buy" Burris from the auction.

On the day of the auction, Flint watched the way the other traders inspected and handled the arms, legs, heads, and bodies of those held captive. He copied their behavior and readied himself for the sale. Burris had no idea who Flint was, but stood tall and proud as he was inspected. When the auctioneer started, he quickly got a bid of five hundred dollars. Flint outbid the other auctioneer by one hundred dollars.

Samuel Burris knew he was doomed when Flint walked over to collect his "property." His heart must have leaped for joy when Flint whispered into Burris's ear, "Thee has been bought with the gold of an abolitionist."

Burris went on to Philadelphia and never again returned to the South. Later, he moved his wife and children to San Francisco, California, where he died in 1869 at the age of sixty-three. Even after moving away, he sent financial support to newly freed slaves.

When I first read this account in its entirety, I was taken not only by the bravery of Hunn and the others but also by their righteousness. The "man-hunter" would have shot and killed the runaways had it not been for Hunn's pacifying intervention. I am reminded of the biblical scripture that instructs the reader to be "as wise as a serpent but as harmless as a dove." Hunn was as suspicious and cautious as he was calm.

One cannot help but be surprised by the number of people who participated in this one act of freedom; the black railroad conductor Burris, the Hunns, the judge, the sheriff's daughter, the constable, Thomas Garrett, the attorney, and the judge all worked together for the freedom of the Hawkins family.

I have often said, "When you walk with purpose, you collide with destiny." John Hunn was a man of purpose who enabled the destiny of others to be fulfilled. Hunn did not want to expose the names of others who worked for the Underground Railroad. He came to know firsthand that the involvement of whites in the abolition of slavery was punishable by law.

John Hunn heard many personal accounts of the horrors of slavery. He kept a journal of those he assisted, but later had it destroyed.

In 1848, for their involvement with the Hawkins family, Hunn and Garrett were sued in the Newcastle Court House under the Fugitive Slave Act and found liable. The law served as a means to fine and punish those who assisted runaways. The loss was tremendous. It caused Hunn to lose his home and all of his inherited property and he was forced to move in with relatives. Still, he continued the fight for freedom. He vowed that he would risk life and limb to bring an end to that horrible institution of slavery.

In 1843, John and Mary's first son, John, had died. Mary died nine years later. John married Anne Jenkins, a cousin by marriage, the following year.

After all of life's hardships and his troubles for assisting runaways, John never stopped his mission. He continued to work up until and after emancipation. In 1870, John and his family moved to St. Helena, South Carolina, and ran a store for the Port Royal Relief Association, which gave assistance to newly freed slaves. His daughter Elizabeth (Lizzie) also taught the blacks on those Sea Islands.

John Hunn returned to Delaware in 1884 and lived there until he died ten years later at the age of seventy-six. On his deathbed, he had his son destroy his journal in front of him.

"Since the actors of the affair are still alive and might be compromised," he said, "it is better to cover the whole episode with oblivion."

While his intentions were noble, sadly, this episode and others like it have been covered with oblivion, a state of being completely forgotten. As if this were not enough, Hunn sacrificed his own legacy for the safety of others. As a result, very little is known or taught of him. Even when I heard his name in my mother's stories, I misrepresented him and the cause he so lovingly fought for. In Shakespeare's *Julius Caesar* we find the lines "The evil that men do lives after them; the good is oft interred with their bones." This was almost the case with John Hunn. I truly believe that we are the living embodiment of the unfulfilled longings of the ancestors.

Hunn's name may not have always been listed and recorded along with that of Harriett Tubman or William Lloyd Garrison, but his work lived long after he did.

I grew up in Wilmington, Delaware, with some of the finest teachers in the country. I studied Shakespeare along with the works of Maya Angelou and Paul Laurence Dunbar. I learned the name of Christopher Columbus's black navigator, Pedro Alonzo Nino, but I did not learn the story of John Hunn. Had I only believed my mother's stories earlier, I might have found him sooner, but sometimes anger and resentment keep us from learning what we need to know. Had I not been so angry at my mother because of her drinking and her treatment of me, I might have listened to her story. Forgiveness is a gift, more for the giver than the receiver. When we let go of the pains we've experienced, we can see more clearly why those pains were inflicted.

John Hunn has enabled me to see not only myself more clearly but also my mother's life and the lives of my ancestors before her.

*Part Three*

# Redemption

You can't separate peace from freedom because no one
can be at peace unless he has his freedom.
—MALCOLM X, 1965

EIGHT

# *Free Your Mind*

Be it enacted, that all and every persons whatsoever who shall
hereafter teach, or cause any slave or slaves to be taught to write, or
shall use or employ any slave as a scribe in any manner of writing
whatsoever . . . every such persons shall for every such offense
forfeit the sum of one hundred pounds current money.

—SOUTH CAROLINA SLAVE CODE, 1740

In the Bible, there is a story of ten lepers who are healed by
Jesus. After they are healed they go on their way. Only one
comes back to say thank you. In the story, Jesus looks about and
asks, "Weren't there nine more?" Then he tells the one who
has returned that because of his faith, he will be made whole.
All ten were healed, but the one who showed gratitude was
made whole and complete.

I am certain that gratitude is a key factor in how well we do in life. My family has been through a great deal, but we have much to be grateful for.

Growing up in Wilmington, Delaware, I knew that education could be my escape, my road to freedom from poverty, abuse, and hardship. Still, like so many young people who live in poverty, I feared being singled out as a "teacher's pet" or a "Goody Two-shoes." Even in the midst of the poverty and chaos in my home, education and knowledge were valued. As bad as my mother could be when she was drinking, television was limited to educational programming, and all outings centered on museums, self-improvement, and black history events. I grew up in the sixties, when black pride was defined by thought rather than style or possessions.

My oldest sister, Myrna, was an artist. Her paintings reflected the beauty and intelligence of African Americans and represented what we should see in ourselves. My sister Christine provided etiquette training and anything having to do with proper grammar. My older brother Brent was next in line and was my tutor in everything cool. My sister Portia was talented in dance, music, and performance and was offered an internship with the world-renowned Alvin Ailey dance troupe. My brother Kevin taught himself to play bass and guitar and knew every chord on any rhythm-and-blues record. I was next in line, and my sister Tanya brought up the rear by reading way before starting preschool and counting every object in sight. We were bright without knowing it, with a natural curiosity for learning and a passion for wanting to know more.

"You may be poor," my mother would say, "but you will never be dirty and there is no reason for ignorance."

I still marvel at the fact that in the midst of real poverty, we had profound intellectual wealth. We were told that having nothing should never translate into being nothing and that poverty was not synonymous with ignorance.

"The Berry name means nothing right now, but it will one day when you give it meaning," my sister Christine would yell.

The contradictions of my home life were nothing in comparison to the ones that existed in the country at that time in the 1960s. It was a time of revolution, free love, peace, and power, but it was also a time of selective inclusion in the black community.

My family was not one of "those" families, nor did anyone believe we had the potential to be. Sociologists point out that if a situation is defined as real, then it becomes real in its consequences. If you tell a child she is nothing, she will act as if she is nothing and will produce very little. For a while I lost my way when I was told by relatives that I was ugly, so I would act that way. I was called stupid, so I made sure that no one thought otherwise. Fortunately for me, there are always those whose sole purpose is to ignite the truth that lies within our hearts.

I was a member of the last all-black graduating class in Wilmington, Delaware. The following school year, 1979, all Wilmington schools were forced by law to integrate. This was twenty-five years after the integration of schools in Little Rock, Arkansas, when nine black children from middle-class families stared directly in the face of America's bigotry. It took attorney Thurgood Marshall, who would later become a Supreme Court justice, to lead the legal battle for change, but it was the images of those young teenagers being tormented by a governor and thousands of adult bigots that enabled the country to see that we were not the evolved nation we pretended to be. Back in 1954, those children were not alone. They had the support of their parents and their community. Additionally, there were others who believed that the nation was ready for change.

My northern city of Wilmington, Delaware, took a lot longer to come around. I remember attending court hearings on the desegregation of public schools. To my surprise, many of my black friends and teachers were dead set against desegregation. They felt that forced integration would cause blacks to lose ground in the battle against oppression, and to a great degree they were correct. Our all-black schools allowed us to study subjects from a black and global perspective. Teachers were not held to the limited and racist views of the school textbooks. While white children in white public schools learned only about the "plight of the Negro" in America, we were taught about all the contributions we'd made to society. I can never sit at a traffic light without thinking of Garrett Morgan, its inventor. When we took trips to see the monuments of Washington, D.C., our focus was on Benjamin Banneker, the black man who helped design the layout for the city's streets.

Much like the black anthropologist Zora Neale Hurston, who grew up in Eatonville, Florida, my educators believed that integration would diminish our power and place in America. Zora was also influenced by an all-black town and schools. She understood that a black man could be mayor; her father had served three terms in that office. When Zora Neale Hurston spoke out against integration in the fifties, people could not understand her reasons for doing so. She was a Barnard College graduate, best-selling author, anthropologist, and professor. Ms. Hurston mingled with the greats of the Harlem Renaissance and dined with members of the white elite. Still, she saw a need for blacks to have their own land and schools and to decide their own fate.

Back in the sixties and seventies, I did not understand why some of my teachers wanted to keep our schools black. I knew from trial integration programs that white schools were much better equipped than my own. I could see that their classrooms had fewer students and teachers were provided with much better resources than in our poor inner-city schools. I wanted what they had. But I understand now why my teachers felt the way they did. They all talked about the importance of meeting the needs of every child; not in the no-child-left-behind way, but in a true sense of doing whatever was necessary to provide for those in need as well as those who were gifted.

My teachers believed that every child had something special, and that it was their calling to bring that gift to light. I went to all-black schools named after lofty white people. My elementary school, George Gray, was named after the Harvard lawyer turned Delaware state attorney general turned senator turned judge for the U.S. Court of Appeals turned presiding judge over the tenth annual conference for international arbitration. In that conference, George Gray declared, "We no longer consider the advance of alien peoples in prosperity as a menace to our own." Gray had no idea that the school named after him would be the starting point for many of Wilmington's black children, who would know nothing of our lofty namesake.

I attended Warner Middle School, named after Emalea Warner, who although she had never attended college founded a committee of women whose purpose it was to arouse public sentiment and convince legislators to create a college for women. I never heard her name mentioned in my history class.

By the time I reached high school, I attended a school named after a Delawarean known throughout the world. Pierre Samuel du Pont was a French writer and economist, and also the father of the founder of the E.I. du Pont de Nemours and Company, one of America's wealthiest businesses of the nineteenth and twentieth centuries.

When I attended these schools, I knew nothing of the people they were named after. Our schools were all black and had educators who centered my education on black culture and black pride.

Atlanta Brown had been my librarian in elementary school, middle school, and high school. She seemed to follow me wherever I went. Ms. Brown was one of the toughest women in my schools. For some reason known only to her and God, she took a liking to me. She would slip me books, and shortly thereafter would ask what I thought of them. She had discovered that beneath my sad exterior, my true passion was books. But I didn't want others to know. My insecurities required that I be tough at all times. One day when I was about thirteen, when no one was looking I returned one of the "by and about black books" that she loved.

"Don't you have any happy black books?" I asked angrily. I had shown no gratitude and even less respect.

Without correcting my attitude, Ms. Brown smiled as if she had spent her whole life waiting for that one question. She turned toward her reference books and, without needing to look for the right one, pulled out a large book that I soon learned was a collection of poems by—who else?—black writers. Again without searching, she flipped to a page and handed it to me. It was a poem by Langston Hughes called "Still Here": "I been scarred and battered / My hopes the wind done scattered . . . I'm still here."

I read it and looked at her, bewildered. She was grinning like she'd won something or knew someone who had.

"That's it?" I asked. "Where's the happy part?" I wondered.

Ms. Brown was ready for this question. She had that knowing look of a wise guru who has waited decades for just one student to ask the one right question.

"It's in the last line," she said. "'I'm still here.' We have all been through a lot," she said in her Southern drawl. "It's up to you to determine what to do with the fact that you are still here."

From that moment until now, words and ideas meant so much more to me.

I've often been accused of being overly analytical and looking too closely at everyday, mundane things. I don't see it that way. I see every moment of life as a gift. I view wisdom and knowledge as liberation. The more I opened my mind to learning, the more Ms. Brown and others were willing to teach me. When I read that our ancestors were punished and put to death for reading, I knew that there was more to learning than I had allowed myself to believe. Reading became an act of revolution, of escape and salvation. The more I learned, the more I needed to learn. I decided that I didn't care who knew it.

There is a belief in the black community that we can be like crabs in a barrel; if one gets close to the top and is able to find its way out, the others will pull him back in. The more serious I became about education, the more I was teased and put down for it. I don't want to believe that we are crabs in a barrel, bent on blocking the progress of anyone trying to make it out. I do know that misery likes company, but not just any company; misery likes miserable company. Those who suffer oppression become so used to it, they are not comfortable with much else.

When I found a way out of poverty through education, many tried to keep me where I was. But, as the scriptures say,

"(S)He who the Son sets free is free indeed." Like John Hunn before me, my transformation was not an outward thing; it ran through my very being and I could not look back. I am grateful beyond measure for everything in my life and, like the one leper who returned to say thank you, I have been made whole.

# NINE

# Go Back to Move Forward

Men will never voluntarily consent to being slaves and they
cannot be held in slavery by physical power, unless they are first
reduced to such deplorable state of ignorance and consequent
helplessness, that they shall neither understand their rights,
nor be able to defend them.

—ELIJAH PORTER BARROWS, *A VIEW OF THE
AMERICAN SLAVERY QUESTION*, 1836

When most Americans think of single black mothers, the
stereotypical image of a twenty-something woman with three
or four children usually comes to mind. These folks don't know
my family. I am the sixth of seven children. My mother had me
at the age of forty-two and my youngest sister, Tanya, at forty-
nine. She was in her late twenties when she had my oldest sis-

ter, Myrna. This was atypical for blacks or whites in the 1940s. My oldest sisters tell wonderful stories of a mother I did not know until I was in my thirties. Back when I was born in 1960, she was already tired of life. I didn't know this then; all I knew was how I felt. When we focus on what is done to us, we become blind to everything else. I am not excusing my mother's behavior; I am simply saying that there was a reason for it.

On the day my mother died, I asked her to help me write this book. It's ironic that on the day of John Hunn's death he asked his son to destroy his journal. Unbeknownst to me, my mother had been writing journals for the last five years of her life. I found them three months after she passed away. On the day she died, she had given me the gift of a clean slate, a new beginning. She had taken the pain of her life and that of the ancestors before her to the other side. Her journals were my second gift, another marker on my journey to true freedom.

I opened the first book on the stack; it was covered in a forest-green carrying case and had the emblem of the New Jersey Educational Opportunity Fund. I recognized it as one of the many binders I've brought home from the conferences that I spoke for. The page was dated November 9, 1999. I was immediately comforted by the familiar handwriting. My mother would keep notes on everything. She would write grocery lists on the inside of broken-down cereal boxes, and would leave notes on grocery store receipts.

"I love you, you are one hell of a woman," one note read. I'd found the note with a hundred dollars that my mother had saved up for my fortieth birthday. For her years of labor, my mother received five hundred dollars a month from Social Security. She would save her meager retirement money for what she called our "rainy days," when things were a little short. What she didn't save or use for rainy days went to her grandchildren.

My mother would send notes and cards with twenty-dollars bills tucked inside. She remembered all the birthdays of every living relative and all of their offspring. Like many women her age, she'd buy enough cards at the beginning of the year to meet the needs of every birthday, anniversary, and holiday throughout the year. Her handwritten notes were also coveted by my friends and their children, who would later recollect the wisdom-filled card that came right when they needed it.

I was tearfully reminded of the timeliness of her words when I first opened her journals. In 1999, in a note to three of my children she wrote:

*William, Jabril and Fatima,*

*Let me tell you a story about your grandmother. Many years ago, when I was a little girl about seven years old, I lived on a farm. My grandfather and grandmother took care of the Big house where the people lived who owned the land that we lived on. Many times my grandmother would take me with her to work. I would watch her do the house work, so I learned how to do many things that I did not learn in school. How to*

*cook, clean, wash clothes, iron clothes and keep a nice house,*
*then I would go out in the field and work with my grandfather,*
*planting vegetables of all kinds. Most of the things we planted*
*would be canned for winter. When it would be very cold with*
*snow on the ground, we would sit around the fire and tell*
*ghost stories. My grandfather would tell the scariest ones. We*
*would be scared to go to bed. We would get under the covers*
*and stay until we went to sleep. The next day would be the*
*same.*

As I sat and read my mother's stories, it was as if she were
sitting next to me reading them herself. Days later when I got
through them, it was as if she'd died again. The woman whom
I had first feared and then loathed and then had come to love
dearly explained her life and her pain. She outlined for me
the journey that led to her bitterness, and the abuse that was
the result. I can't tell her story in its entirety. There are many
aspects of her life that would be painful to the living; this was
not her intent. Her goal was to leave a legacy of strength, wisdom, and love. Many of the passages were written directly to
me. She somehow knew that I would need them to continue
this story.

My mother was born in 1918, the same year as Sam Walton,
Pearl Bailey, Howard Cosell, Rita Hayworth, and Anwar Sadat.
My mother, whose life was scarred by abuse, poverty, and ne-
glect, outlived them all. She was born the same year that World
War I ended, the war in which the all-black 369th Infantry

Regiment won France's Croix de Guerre for their bravery in battle. None of the infantry ever retreated nor were they ever captured. During that same war, however, just a year before my mother's birth, sixty-four men from the 24th Infantry were court-martialed in Texas after seventeen white gang members were killed when they attacked black soldiers.

The year 1918 was also when, under President Woodrow Wilson, the Sedition Act was passed, making it illegal to use "disloyal, profane or abusive language about the U.S. Government, the flag or armed forces in times of war."

My mother was born four years before the beginning of the Harlem Renaissance, and nine years after W.E.B. Du Bois established the NAACP. One of the top-grossing films in 1918 was *Tarzan*, a movie in which Africans were depicted as savages but played by white men. My mother was born in a year when an international war ended but fighting between blacks and whites in the United States was in full swing. She was somewhat sheltered by the love and lessons of her grandparents, but would later become fully aware of the hatred outside in the world. She wrote the following on November 9, 1999:

> *Another thing I want to tell you, I don't think you will ever read in a history book. When we moved in town, we lived on Water Street in Dover, Delaware. Two houses from where we lived was a prison. They had a whipping post. People that got caught stealing were tied to the post and whipped. In another town not far away, people would get tarred and feathered with*

*hot tar. Many things you should know about the hardships of*
*your people.*

My mother had her own hardships as well. She did not
know her own mother until she was thirteen, and she met her
father years later. She was raised by Annie Mae and John
Henry Freeman, her grandparents. According to my mother,
John Henry Freeman was the kindest man who ever walked the
earth. He was black and Native American. Tall and lean with
smooth black skin, he wore his hair parted down the center
with two long braids that hung down his back. Aside from his
storytelling, John Henry Freeman said very little, and when he
spoke, he spoke softly. He was a hard worker and a good storyteller. He would tell his stories at night to entertain their thirteen children, my mother, and her two cousins. There were
other families nearby who would sometimes join them on
weekends for story time.

Sometimes travelers, or "hobos," as my mother called
them, would come to their home for food and to camp out.
"Old John Henry wouldn't turn anybody away," she said.

According to my mother, Annie Mae, her grandmother,
was another story. "She was full of fire and didn't take nothing .
off of nobody." When the children misbehaved or "got out of
line," it was Annie Mae who doled out the punishments.

*One day my grandmother sent me to the store which was five*
*miles down the road to get sugar. I took eggs in exchange for*

*the sugar. I got the sugar and had five cents left, so I got a large*
*Lolly pop. No one said I could spend the five cents. So here I am*
*again, in big trouble.*

"Annie Mae was mean," my mother once told me. She said
it had to do with the fact that Annie Mae's mother was part
white and part black because her mother had been raped by
her slaveholder. Her father was Cherokee but Annie could pass
for white. Annie's mother had had a harsh life and she passed
it on to her daughter, Caroline, my mother's mother. Later on,
when my mother was near death, she took back her words, or
rather explained them.

"Annie Mae wasn't mean," she said. "She was sad."

Whatever punishments Annie doled out, John Henry tried
to make up for them.

"We would sit close and listen to his stories," she said. "He
could really tell a good story. And his ghost stories made you
afraid to sleep at night."

*"Long time ago, there was man 'round here with one good*
*arm and one bad one. The bad one just hung by his side like it*
*was dead. Every now again, the bad arm would get to*
*working, but it only did bad things. Nobody ever knew when*
*that bad arm would act up, not even the man. But when it got*
*to twitching, you knew you better get to running. One day*
*when he was alone in the field, that arm got to twitching.*
*Now that man knew he had to stand still when it did, cause if*

*he stood real still, that arm might settle down on its own.
Well, that day he stood still as a rock. That arm twitched and
shook, it twitched and shook, then all of a sudden, that arm
ripped itself right out of the socket and went off into the field.
Now I don't know if it's true, but they say that arm is still out
there and it's still looking for a bad child. If it finds one it will
do to you all the bad things you do to somebody else. If you see
that arm, don't run, just stand still as a rock and just maybe
it won't get you."*

My mother loved John Henry's stories. When I was still a
girl, I would hear her tell them to other relatives. They would
laugh about how afraid they had been and how they believed
that the stories were true. Back when I was a kid listening to
"grown folks," I was afraid.

My mother said that John Henry didn't believe a child
should be beaten. There was only one time John Henry spanked
my mother. She laughed whenever she told the story about the
time when she and her cousin were supposed to take the cow
out to pasture but didn't.

"It was our chore to take the cow to pasture every morning
before we went to school. There was only one school in Lebanon and it was far. It was a one-room house and we had to
take the cow to the field, then double back in the other direction for school. One day my cousin said it would be easier if we
just put the cow in the church. So, that's what we did."

When my mother talked about this incident her eyes would

light up and she would laugh like a girl. She wrote about the incident in her journal to my children.

*One day on our way to school, my cousin and I decided to put the two cows that we walk to pasture, in an old church that belonged to Quakers. They used it once a year, so we put them in the church. On our way home from school we was to pick them up. Not that day. The cows had really messed up that church and was gone. Now you talk about being scared to death. We were out of sight. [We hid.] Of course you can guess what happened to me and my cousin.*

*Some weeks later, we could play for a little while outside like bring in the wood for the fireplace and kitchen stove, milk the cows and feed the horse and chickens and all the other things we had on the farm. And that was getting to play outside.*

"John Henry Freeman really gave us what for that day," she told me.

Years later, when I drove my mother to Lebanon, Delaware, where their farm had been, we passed a small building in the middle of the field.

"That's it, that's it!" she said. "That's the church where we put the cows. They tore up that place. I can't believe it's still standing."

On closer inspection, I learned that the small building was not really a church at all; it was the Quaker meeting house that John Hunn and his family attended.

When I began to do research for this book, I hunted through records and documents until I found my family. My mother was still living then but I had not yet found her journals. Still, I had her stories and the records of John Hunn and his family. I was able to locate the names among the census data of 1870.

The first federal census of the United States was taken on August 2, 1790. However, five of the states' reports were destroyed sometime between 1790 and 1830. Delaware was one of the five; the others were Georgia, Kentucky, New Jersey, and Virginia. The census of 1870 was the ninth census of the United States and only the second to include Native Americans, but only those who renounced their tribal laws. This was only five years after the abolition of slavery in this country. The counting of African Americans as something other than the property of a white household was still new. I was not able to locate my relatives prior to the census of 1870; it was only after finding John Hunn and the location of the Hunn family property that I could find the Freemans.

Fortunately for me, my mother was still alive to verify and "correct" the information. In the late 1800s, census takers, or enumerators, would come around to gather information from whites; they would also take account of his "property," the slaves he owned and, after slavery, the blacks who lived on his land. In 1870 after emancipation, enumerators were to record the birthplace, birth date, gender, "color," profession or trade, value of real estate, whether mother and father were married, those who could not read, those who could write, whether deaf, dumb, or blind, insane or "idiotic." Much of this information was not recorded for my family. I did learn from the data, however, that all of the members listed in my great-grandfather's household could read. Listed in the census data were my grandmother Caroline and her sisters Elizabeth and Mary, but there were more children born to them at that time who were not listed. According to my mother, Annie and John Henry Freeman had thirteen children.

"For some reason, some of their children lived down the way on another farm," my mother said.

She didn't know the reason for the separation and could conjecture only that maybe there was a relative or friend who needed their hands in the field. When I asked my mother their names and what had become of them she said that she didn't know. At this point in my mother's illness, I learned to allow her to tell our family story as it came to her and that if I pressed too much for answers she became frustrated and somewhat distressed.

"Why can't I remember their names?" she'd ask. "There was Lizzie and Ruth, Mary, oh, I don't know."

My mother underwent surgery and had the tumor removed. After her recovery she was like her old self, smiling, doing laundry, and telling family stories.

I relied on her stories and the census data to help put together the pieces of the Freeman journey. Still, there were many gaps and unanswered questions. What I did learn was that John Henry Freeman was a sharecropper and an overseer on the Hunn family farm. His birth date is still a mystery to me. In the census data of 1870, it is recorded that the overseer named John Henry was born in 1863. This could not have been true; he would have been seven at the time, with children who were older than him. It is possible that the census taker made a mistake. It is also possible that John Henry had a son with the same name who was listed as the overseer instead of his father.

The census of 1880, just ten years later, records John Henry Freeman's age as forty-nine, which would have made him eighty-seven when my mother was born. This is possible but not likely.

There are other mistakes in those records. For example, my great-grandmother Annie is listed as John Henry's daughter, while his daughter Lizzie is listed as his wife.

I have asked older relatives what they can recall of my mother's aunts and uncles, and have found that they know even less than I do. My sister Christine was amazed to learn that my mother had so many aunts and uncles.

"She never talked to me much about her life after Caroline," Christine said. "As a matter of fact, she didn't talk that much about Caroline."

Even though I knew there were inconsistencies in the census data and I could not get all the information I needed from family sources, when I found the names of my relatives listed in the documents, I felt as if my ancestors were all standing right there with me. I copied the information and read the names of my great-aunts and -uncles to my mother and she just cried. I cried with her. I could see that she had been right all along. John Henry Freeman had been a part of the Hunn family and John Hunn was a part of the Freemans. It is possible that he was there on the day that the Hawkins family came riding in looking for help.

When I asked my mother if she ever heard tales of runaway slaves she laughed and said, "You really don't listen, do you? I told you that Granddad said that he and John Hunn was always running folk."

I could not recall hearing this story. But since I had a hard time comprehending that our family was free during slavery and was determined to negate the idea that John Hunn was a nice man and not a slave owner, it is easy now for me to believe that my mother had told the story and I had not listened.

Once I opened myself to my mother's stories, she opened her heart to tell them.

"They would sneak folks through in the nights, and sometimes broad daylight," my mother said. "Granddaddy said it was hard times, but that just meant that good was coming."

My family still holds to the belief that hard times foreshadow the good that lies ahead.

"All the Hunns were good people," my mother said. "People talked about how good they were all the way up to Wilmington."

She said that John Henry took the last name Freeman because he wanted everyone to know that he was truly free. I found a document of a petition for freedom by a man from

Delaware named John Henry arguing that he was "unlawfully took." Because I do not know John Henry's birth date, I do not know for certain if the petitioner is in fact my great-grandfather or one of his relatives. I know from my mother's stories that John Henry was "free and then he wasn't, but then he was free again."

"That's how we got the name Freeman," she loved to say. "'Cause Granddaddy wanted everybody to know that he was free."

It is possible that John Henry's freedom was questioned when the Hunns lost their property. It is also likely that his participation with the abolitionist movement temporarily cost him his freedom. I do not know. I do know that his customs and beliefs still live within my family, and that his desire to end oppression is a part of the fabric of my being.

My great-grandparents taught my mother many of the lessons she passed on to me.

We have odd traditions and beliefs, many of which I have not found elsewhere. When a person comes to my home for the first time, he or she must use the front door, even though the side door is more convenient. My siblings and I were never allowed to say thank you for meals or clothing, or for having our hair combed. We were taught instead to say, "I appreciate you." If anyone in my family gets a fever, we put chopped onions in his or her socks. I do not know how this works, I just know that it does. In less than one hour, the fever is broken, and the house smells of fried onions.

Whenever I asked my mother why we had to do these

things, she would say, "I don't know, that's what we always did."

Some things that were mere superstitions among black folks were taboo for my mother: you should cut your hair only on a full moon, never ever talk in a storm, and when speaking of the dead, always lower your voice.

My mother's religious beliefs were very similar to those of Native Americans, Africans, and the Society of Friends. She too believed that God dwells in the hearts of people and that all people are the same. She believed in hard work, caring for those who were less fortunate and in need, and that you must show appreciation for all things. These were the lessons she learned from her grandparents, John Henry and Annie Mae Freeman. It is possible that they were also the ways of those early Native Americans, the ones the Dutch tried to use as slaves. With their Native American heritage, John Henry and Annie Mae must have come in contact with the lessons and customs of native folks. During slavery, blacks and Native Americans shared similar hardships and forged bonds as a result. It is believed among researchers that most of the African customs of those enslaved were whitewashed from the lives of Delaware blacks. Having little contact with other Africans, it was hard for them to maintain their cultural uniqueness. However, others believed that our African traditions were kept alive in our music, our spirituality, and our storytelling. The role of Griot, or storyteller, was the role my grandfather played. I wish I knew more of his stories and of he and Annie Mae's life.

Still, I know that the spirit of folks and their blood memories connect us to our ancestry and to one another. It allows us
to meet someone for the first time and feel connected to him
or her. Our heritage and history are more than documents and
census figures; they are fact and feeling, and cry out to be remembered. When we remember our ancestors and their stories, we light a pathway for our own journey to spiritual,
emotional, and intellectual freedom.

TEN

# The Aftermath

John Henry Freeman was not a slave. I don't know how he came
to be free, but according to my mother he was free most of his
life. It's amazing to me that I don't have to go back far to find
ancestors who were slaves. My mother was born fifty-three
years after slavery ended and was raised by her grandparents,
who had seen it up close. John Henry lived on the farm and
worked for the Hunns before their home was taken as part of
the settlement in the lawsuit for assisting the Hawkins family
to freedom.

My great-grandfather lived until 1929 or 1930. Shortly after my mother moved out to live with her mother, Caroline,
John Henry passed away, and Annie Mae followed him a month
later. When I asked her how old he was, she simply said, "Real,
real old," and that no one knew for certain. Longevity runs in
our family.

When my grandmother Caroline died, we all believed that
she was in her sixties; we found out later that she was actually
in her nineties. Caroline had porcelain-smooth skin and jet-
black hair that had never been dyed. The county building that
held her birth certificate had burned down. When it did, my
grandmother fabricated a new birth date and had new documents made to match it. Wc still laugh about the lie and how
her looks supported the claim.

 I don't know why my mother was not aware that Caroline
was her mother until she came to take her away. She never told
me nor did she write about it. I do know that this was a very
painful event in my mother's history. There are numerous accounts of children growing up believing their mother is their
sister and they learn the truth much later. This was not the case
for my mother. She did not know or even recognize Caroline.

When she came to take my mother to live with her in the big
city of Dover and then Wilmington, my mother said she
thought she was being taken by a strange white woman. The little thirteen-year-old had no idea what was going on. She cried
to John Henry and Annie Mae, and begged to stay, telling them
she would be good and would do everything right.

"John Henry just went out to the field," she said.

My mother knew that her grandparents didn't want her to go, but, for some reason unknown to her, they couldn't put a stop to it. She cried for weeks and had a hard time dealing with the change. Prior to that time, she had not even thought about her mother or father and felt that she "belonged to" John Henry and Annie Mae. Fortunately for her and for me, John Henry Freeman had given her his wisdom, while Annie Mae had passed on her spirit and fire. Later on, their lessons would take my mother through situations where she would be scarred and battered, but never broken. She wrote this advice to her grandchildren in her journal:

> I talk about my grandfather a lot because I loved him very much. My grandparents were the only ones who cared for me. Granddad would fuss at me and tell me the right things to do, but he loved me. I needed to hear all the things he told me about life. Sometimes, I hated what he tried to tell me, but later on in life, I found out that he was so right. That's why I want you to listen to your mother and do the things she tells you to do. Learn from what she tells you. It is never wrong. I have been there and done all the wrong things in life. Don't do it ever. Try to stay focused. Believe in yourself and be kind. Above all, God is and will be there when all your friends are gone. Love will keep you. Don't forget to love. Know that I love you very much and want you to do your best.

# ELEVEN

# Sometimes I Feel Like
# a Motherless Child

The tendency of the slave system is in every way injurious to
the slave-holding part of the community. One of its deplorable
effects is to blunt the moral sensibilities of the master. . . .
Another is to encourage licentiousness. . . . A female slave
has no protection against the white man.

—ELIJAH PORTER BARROWS

When my mother went to live with her mother, Caroline
Freeman, she felt alone and afraid. She was my grandmother's
only child then and had no other playmates. On the farm, she
had been accustomed to running freely and playing with other
relatives. My mother never drove a car, but she could ride a
horse bareback.

"We would stand on the railing of the front porch and

jump right on that horse. Then we would take off riding," she said.

She played with the toys her grandfather made for her, and she even had her own seesaw. When she moved to Dover and then on to Wilmington, it was just her and Caroline, who before then she hadn't known at all. From my mother's journals, I have learned that once she left the farm, she was forced to go to work. She wrote the following in 2000:

> *I often look around and see how blessed you children are. You have a very loving mother. I did not have that when I was growing up.*
>
> *When my grandmother told me she was not my mother, I did not know what to say. You see I called my mother Nanny and I thought that meant mother. I knew my grandmother had thirteen children. Some were twins. But this nearly white woman could not be my mother. When I went with my mother I hated her. The first thing she did was get me a job at an undertakers [house]. I did not like him at all. His wife was very nice, she was a school teacher. I made three dollars a week. I had to be there five days a week. Every day was hell.*

She worked as a housekeeper for a prominent white family. My mother was just thirteen at the time, the same age I was when I starting cleaning banks after school and private homes in the mornings and on weekends. The difference for me, though, was that I got to go back home when I was done.

My mother lived with the family she worked for and went home only on Saturdays. The woman of the house was kind, but the man—the undertaker—was not.

There are some things about my mother's life that I needed to know—they have helped me to get a better understanding of her and her motivations—but there are some things that were just too hard to learn. This is one of those things.

When my mother was just thirteen and didn't have anyone nearby to tell it to, that undertaker took her to the basement where he did his work and raped her.

"The family had a cat and that cat sat there watching the whole thing," she wrote.

It was not until I read this in her journal that I understood her hatred of cats. Once my sister Myrna had gotten a Siamese kitten and my mother refused to visit her.

"She knows that I don't like no damned cats," she said.

My mother had projected her hatred for that man onto the cat, the only witness to the crime. When she told Caroline what happened, my grandmother refused to believe her.

"Who would want your black ass?" my grandmother had said.

We still don't know why Caroline was so bitter and angry. It's possible that it had to do with the schism between her and her parents. My mother had nothing but loving praise for them. Even Annie Mae, the offspring of the rape between a slave owner and her enslaved mother, who could be tough at times, especially when giving a punishment, earned my mother's respect and appreciation. This was not the case with Caroline. The only clue to my grandmother's anger comes from my mother's stories about how Caroline was always sickly. Prolonged illnesses can take a toll on your body and spirit. The fact that my mother did not know Caroline and thought that she was being taken away by a white woman indicates that there was a rift in the Freeman family.

The birth of my mother could not have been the cause of her problem with my grandparents, at least not from their perspective. To them all children were a blessing; they cherished my mother.

My oldest living sister, Christine, actually cringes when she talks about Caroline.

"Did you ever hear about the time when Caroline closed and locked Mom into an outhouse and then set it on fire?" Christine once asked.

This was not one of the stories my mother told me, nor had she written about it in her journals.

"What?" I asked in disbelief. I told my sister that I had never heard about this and that it seemed harsh even for Caroline. I asked Christine what had led her to do such a thing, but she said that she never found out.

Fortunately, a relative heard Mom's screams and got her out before she was physically injured, but the emotional damage had already been done.

My mother's rape by the undertaker evoked no feelings of sympathy from Caroline. She found the strength to refuse to go back to work, so Caroline beat her. Still, she would not return. Eventually, Caroline was able to get my mother to go back to "apologize" to the woman for not going to work and to tell her that she would not be coming back. When she did, the woman told her that she understood why she did not want to come back. The woman cried and said that her husband was not a good man. The woman gave Caroline money for my mother's "trouble," and that was the end of it.

You would think that once she heard the truth, Caroline would have apologized to my mother for not believing her. Instead, she blamed her for the man's behavior.

"You were probably all up in his face," Caroline said to her.

I will always be appalled by the women who take the side of an abuser over that of their own child. I can understand that a woman's self-worth can be diminished to the point of turning on other women; still, I have a difficult time understanding how anyone can think that a rape victim could have ever initiated her own attack.

Within a few days, Caroline sent my mother to work for another family; tragically, the same thing happened. That time, though, no one believed my mother and the abuse continued until the wife caught the man in the act and fired my mother for "trying to have an affair with her husband."

The effects of slavery have had an impact on all of society. White boys, who grew up believing that they could do whatever they wanted to a black woman, taught the same thing to their sons. All women have had to suffer from this behavior. We are all connected, even in our pain.

"People can be cruel," my mother used to say. "But for every mean person, there is a good one trying to do the right thing."

TWELVE

# Family Ties

For Sale
6 Negro slaves
Two men, 35 years and 50 years old; two boys, 12 and 18 years old
Two mulatto wenches, 40 and 30 years old
We will sell all together to the same party but will not separate.

—AUCTION POSTER, 1849

I have previously mentioned that my great-grandparents had thirteen children. To John Henry and Annie Mae Freeman, children were a blessing. My mother grew up alongside her aunts, uncles, and cousins, and all of them were treated the same. So much so that when I showed her census data of her family, she was not certain which family member was an aunt or a cousin. I have also come to discover that relatives I believed to be aunts or uncles were really third or fourth cousins. My own children are my maternal nieces and nephews.

This is very common in the black community. We have a reverence for family that goes beyond close blood ties. Still, I was amazed when I located my mother's father's family in the same census data; they had lived down the road from my mother's family but were sharecroppers on the same farm. My mother's father was Marva Demby. His family and my mother's had been neighbors. The Dembys and Freemans related to one another as family. My mother referred to the Demby children as cousins, and the parents as aunt and uncle. When I found them listed in the census data, I asked who they were. My mother excitedly recalled details of the names that I read out loud to her, and told me that they were family.

"Oh, yeah," she said. "Anna and Sarah lived down the road from us. They had children who played right along with me. They were like relatives."

I asked her how her relatives could have also been her father's family.

"Not blood relatives," she said with indignation. "They were our people, like you and Bernita," she said, referring to my friend and sister Bernita Berry.

Bernita and I went to graduate school together and shared a last name. Everyone assumed we were sisters and we became such. Most black people have "family members" who are not related by blood. In many cases, these nonrelated "relatives" are closer than those who are connected by blood. These relations are often so close that after a few generations, no one knows that they are not truly related.

Marva Demby and my grandmother Caroline were not married. My mother knew who her father was, but did not have much contact with him. After she left the farm, she had no further connection to his family. My family and I believe that this had more to do with Caroline than it did with Marva Demby.

After I wrote about my family in *I'm on My Way but Your Foot Is on My Head: A Black Woman's Story of Getting Over Life's Hurdles*, I was at a book signing when one of the Demby family members came up and welcomed me into the fold. She also invited me to an upcoming family reunion. I was excited and called my mother to tell her about it; it would be great for us to go together, I told her.

"They didn't want me when I needed them, so I sure don't want them now," my mother said. She said that although the Dembys were like family when she was a child, after she grew up she had little contact with them.

I tried to explain to her that they probably didn't know who she was or what her life had been like, and that we should do as she had often suggested—let the past stay in the past—but my mother wasn't hearing it. There is more to the my-mother-not-knowing-her-father story, but she did not share it with me. My siblings knew even less than I did about my mother's parentage. Based on the fact that she did not even recognize her own mother when she came to get her at the age of thirteen, it is more than likely that Caroline played a major role in keeping my mother and her father apart. It is also likely that Caroline's behavior is a result of something that happened between her and Marva.

I respected my mother's feelings and did not go to the Demby family reunion. Since she has passed away and gave me the gift of a clean slate, I feel that she would now want me to go, that my mother would want me to reconnect to that part of her.

The system of slavery and those who maintained it sought to tear families apart. It did whatever was necessary to keep those who were enslaved in fear and in total submission.

In the narrative *Reflection of My Slavery Days*, William Henry Singleton wrote in 1922:

> *Breaking up families and the parting of the children from their parents was quite common in the slavery days . . . [but] slaves were as fond of their children as white folks. But nothing could be done about it for the law said we were only things and had no more rights under the law than animals. I believe it was only the more cruel Masters who separated families.*

While most slave owners thought nothing of separating families, there are some accounts of slaveholders who would not separate family members.

In the narrative of Thomas Smallwood, published by James

Stephens in 1851, he tells of how he and his sister were together "willed" to the wife of the Reverend J. B. Ferguson. The will required that Smallwood and his sister be set free when he was thirty and she was twenty-five. However, Ferguson (not being a friend of slavery) paid for Smallwood and his sister's freedom before then. Smallwood "hired" himself out for sixty dollars a year until the debt was paid back to Ferguson.

Smallwood was also taught to read and write in the household at which he was hired: "He employed many servants about his house; he hired all; for it to be said to his credit and humanity, he would own no slaves, although living in a slave holding country."

For me, even this is a small act of rebellion against the institution of slavery. If we are to move beyond the bonds of slavery, we must recognize even the slightest acts of resistance that occurred during that time. Only then will we be able to mend and move forward.

The slave code dictated that a person of bondage could not own anything, including her own children. A child born in slavery did not belong to the father or mother, but to the master. By law, a black child took the condition of the mother. This way, even if the father was free, the child would still be owned by the mother's master. One can't help but see the impact that this has had on present family connections, or the lack thereof, of black folks. Still, black parents who lived and suffered through slavery understood the need to be connected to one another and did whatever was necessary to keep the bond strong. There were others who worked to keep families together.

It is painful to me now that so many of my own family members are lost to me. It is important in our journey toward liberation that we reconnect the family ties.

# THIRTEEN

# Family Matters, Color Counts

If it had not been for storytelling,
the black family would not have survived.

—JACKIE TORRENCE

Family relations have always been a difficult subject for me. Large families are bound to be fraught with discord, regardless of the socioeconomic background or level of education. Within my family, there are difficulties among siblings and also among cousins, aunts, and uncles. When my mother moved from the farm to live with Caroline, she was still her only child. Later on, Caroline had a son and two more daughters.

I hardly knew my uncle Sonny. He would come around on

holidays from time to time, but I did not know much about him. In fact, it was not until he was robbed and murdered that I found out that he was my mother's blood brother.

Until then, I had assumed that he was someone we called "uncle" out of respect, not a real relative. Uncle Sonny was a mean drunk and the family outsider. He was lean and very dark. His features were more West African than the Native American or white features of his grandparents, mother, and siblings. They all had long straight hair and much lighter skin. My mother, who wasn't very dark at all, was the darkest of the girls. For this, and her preference for very dark men, she also became a family outsider.

Visits to my grandmother were rather memorable, but not in a good way. Whenever we visited Grandmom, we had to be our cleanest clean. The visits were stressful for my mother. Our clothes were cleaned and pressed and every hair had to be in place. In her later years, my grandmother Caroline developed glaucoma and as a result went completely blind. My siblings and I would laugh about the fact that everything had to be perfect.

"She's blind, she can't even see us," we would whisper. "How will she know what we look like?" we wondered.

"Oh, believe you me, she will know," my mother would answer, hearing everything we ever said.

We would arrive at my grandmother's house and line up in order of age, the oldest to the youngest, and my grandmother would inspect us.

"These must be Bea's kids," she would say.

At first, I thought she knew us by the smells of the soap and Dixie Peach hair grease that had been smoothed into our scalp. I learned otherwise when I asked her how she knew who we were.

"Y'all the blackest grandkids I got," she said, referring to our dark skin. Someone must have told her that we were dark, unlike my cousins, who were much lighter than we were. They had hazel or green eyes and straight hair. She added insult to injury by telling me that I was the fattest and blackest of all.

I didn't get too upset, though, because she would hand each of us a nickel. Back then a nickel went a long way in penny candy. Most of my favorites, like Bit-O-Honey and Jaw Breakers, were two for a penny. We would run off, happy to have gotten the nickel. Years later my sister Chris told me that all the other cousins got five-dollar bills.

When I did my dissertation for my doctoral degree, I studied the subject of colorism, black-on-black discrimination. I wanted to learn more about the colorism that existed in my family. I already understood the hardships that came with being "too dark," and was not surprised when the research supported those beliefs. The real surprise came when I discovered that the very light received the same amount of discrimination as the very dark from other black people. Lighter blacks were also ostracized and put down for being "too light." By that time, my grandmother had been dead for more than ten years, but I started to understand the reasons for some of her behavior.

Blacks have discriminated against one another since slavery, due in part to the differential treatment of slaveholders toward so-called mulattoes and the children the slaveholders themselves fathered. However, it is a popular misconception that lighter slaves were always preferred. In *The Underground Railroad*, William Still tells the story of Cornelius Scott, a "mulatto" who had been "very much bleached by the Patriarchal system" and would pass for white: "Although a young man only twenty three years of age, and quite stout, his fair complexion was decidedly against him."

Scott felt that his lighter skin color worked against him. While there are certainly stories of light blacks being given "preferential" treatment, this is often due to the fact that enslaved blacks who were lighter in skin color were also the offspring of the slaveholders. In the case of "former slave" William Singleton, being the offspring of the slaveholder's brother was the very reason he was sold away from his family: "I learned . . . the reason I was sold was because there had been trouble between my master and his brother over me and my presence was continually reminding them of something they wanted to forget."

Another misconception is that enslaved blacks were deliberately separated by color for work duties, with lighter blacks working in the house while the darker servants worked the fields. This is not completely true. In most instances, slaves who worked in the house were also forced to work in the fields. The division of labor was determined by the size of the plantation, the number of slaves, the crops that were planted, and the time of year, or season, of the crops that had been planted. When there were large fields to be harvested, all of the enslaved, including children, were forced to work until the work was done. Even in the case of the small plantations, enslaved workers had duties in all areas. It is true that some of those enslaved children who had been fathered by the slave owner served as playmates to the slave owner's "white" children; however, as soon as that child was old enough to work the fields, usually at age seven, he did so.

Mixed-race children were sometimes promised freedom when their slaveholder father passed away, only to find that this promise of freedom would not be granted. Some states even made it illegal to grant manumission to a child fathered by a white man, arguing that the child took the status of the mother, not the father.

I am reminded again of my mother's insight that "The law is for the lawless." It becomes obvious that the law was necessary because there were those who tried to free others or themselves using their white parentage as an escape route.

This was the case of husband and wife William and Ellen Craft, whose "most interesting case of escape" appeared in the *Liberator Newspaper* in 1849. A published letter from William Wells Brown to William Lloyd Garrison gives the details of this remarkable escape:

*Ellen is so near white, that she can pass without suspicion
for a white woman. Her husband is much darker. He is a me-
chanic, and by working nights and Sundays, he laid up money
enough to bring himself and his wife out of slavery . . . Ellen
dressed in men's clothing, and passed as the master, while her
husband passed as the servant. In this way, they traveled from
Georgia to Philadelphia.*

In *The Underground Railroad* by William Still, the escape of
John Wesley Gibson of Taylor's Mount, Maryland, is reported.
Gibson was white enough to pass and, "having resolve to serve
no longer as a slave," concluded to "hold his head up and put
on airs," escaping to Baltimore, where he found he could pass
for white. He reported that prior to escaping to freedom, his
"master" held the reins on him rather tightly. Apparently,
Gibson looked so much like his father, he was not permitted to
leave the plantation, fearing that others would realize his father's "misdeeds."

While lighter skin often provided passage to freedom, it
was not always preferred by blacks. My own doctoral dissertation illustrated how lighter blacks are often treated poorly because of their color.

I believe that my grandmother Caroline's treatment toward
my mother and her children was due in part to the treatment
of other blacks toward her. She was light enough to pass for
white at a time when it was "beneficial" to do so, but she chose
not to. Her love toward her own people had to be strong

enough for her to stay within the black community, a community that did not fully embrace her. I have learned that she was highly respected, feared, and admired in her community, but always referred to by her light complexion. Surely, this had an impact.

In addition to color, there are other family issues that have been carried from one generation to the next. Like my mother, I too grew up without a father. I grew up in a black community where there was a father in almost every home. Still, I did not know my own. Deprivation is difficult, but relative deprivation carries its own scars. If you don't have something that everyone around you has, the lack seems even greater.

When I was a child I did not have anyone to call father, but worse still, I was not allowed to talk about it. There were things in the Berry household we just did not discuss, and not having a father was one of them. I knew that my mother had been married to my oldest brother Brent's father. His name was Richard Berry, which is how I got the name. But I am not a Berry by blood. Richard Berry passed away long before I was born, but we all got his name. To this day when I meet people with the same last name, I allow all of the questions that are asked when folks are trying to determine whether or not they are related to you.

"Where are your people originally from?" they ask. "We had some Berrys in the Delaware, Pennsylvania area, and I bet we are related," they say, smiling, like a long-lost relative.

Once when I met the beautiful actress Halle Berry, I was amazed when she did the same thing.

"Do people ever ask you if you're related to me?" she asked. I did the only thing an insecure, fatherless kid from Delaware could do. I laughed, loudly. Halle wanted to know why I was laughing.

"Look at you," I said. "You are gorgeous."

I silently wondered how anyone could have ever thought that the two of us were related. She was tall and lean with skin the color of caramel. I was short and dark and not lean. Halle must have known what I felt and had probably felt some of it herself.

"Look at you," she said back to me. "You're gorgeous too."

"Well, we must be related, then," I told her, smiling.

You've got to love Halle.

Still, I know the truth. I am a Berry in name only. The whole name thing among many African Americans is an interesting point. In some families, siblings often have different last names, each one being named after their own father. During the 1960s and 1970s some African Americans changed their names to names that originated in Africa, where their ancestors were from. During the Civil Rights era and the Black Power Movement, some folks shunned their surnames, believing that their last name was that of a slave owner. But I found out when researching this book that this wasn't always the case. Many emancipated and runaway blacks changed their names as soon as they got to freedom. When John Henry Hill escaped from an auction sale in Richmond, Virginia, in 1853, he made his way to Canada and was given the instruction that many fugitives were given: "Change your name, and never tell anyone how you escaped."

When I read William Still's book and other narratives of former slaves, I was amazed by the letters that were often signed with two names, such as Emma Brown (alias Mary Epps), Robert Jackson (alias Wesley Harris), and Romulus Hall (alias George Weemes).

Fugitives often changed their names following the advice of the Philadelphia committee, a group of abolitionists who provided financial, emotional, and spiritual support.

Many free blacks took their father's name as a last name. A most interesting case is that of the history of Benjamin Banneker, America's first political appointee under Thomas Jefferson. He was a publisher, astronomer, clock maker, and surveyor of the District of Columbia. Banneker was the grandson of Molly Walsh, a European immigrant indentured to servitude for seven years. At the end of her term of service, Molly bought a farm near Baltimore along with two slaves. She later freed them and married one of them, a man known as Banna Ka. Banna Ka later changed his name to Bannaky, the name that became the family name of his children, including Mary Bannaky, Benjamin's mother. When Mary Bannaky grew up she also purchased a slave, Robert, whom she later freed and married. Robert and Mary were the parents of the boy Benjamin, whose Quaker schoolteacher changed the spelling of his name to Banneker.

The taking of a father's name as a new surname was common among fugitives and former slaves.

When I was a child, I actually prayed for a father. I knew that I had to have one out there somewhere. I hoped that one day he would come and make me feel special. I did not want the name Berry; it was my brother Brent's name. Like newly freed blacks I wanted the name of my father.

My sister Portia not only knew her father, she got to spend holidays and summers with him. Every summer she was packed up and sent to enjoy the life of her father Emerson's family. She would come back with new clothes, toys, and stories of adventures that I could only dream of. That relative deprivation was staring at me again. If the summers weren't enough, I had to deal with those holidays when Emerson would bring his entire family to spend time with us in our poverty. As my mother said, "We were poor, but we were clean." Well, Emerson's clan downright sparkled. He drove a nice big car that seemed to be replaced with a newer model on each trip. Every major holiday, Emerson, his wife, and their son and daughter would drive from Washington, D.C., to spend the holiday with Portia. There were always presents, but none were for me or my other siblings; they were all for Portia. My mother had let Emerson know that if he wanted to see his daughter on holidays, he would have to come to her. I still marvel at the fact that Emerson's wife went along with this arrangement.

We'd all crowd around our small dining room table for

Thanksgiving, Christmas, and Easter dinners. It was like a page out of Alice Walker's *The Color Purple*, where exes and in-laws sat talking about their former lives together. My siblings and I would watch Portia open one present after the other, wishing that any one of them was for us. Relative deprivation really is relative, and in this case it was downright cruel. I secretly longed for a father who would come and bring me presents while Portia was forced to watch. I wanted a father who would take me away from the poverty to rescue me from my mother's drinking and the subsequent verbal and physical abuse that started around age nine or ten and lasted until I left for college.

It was not to be.

But even without a father, I got to college. It was around that time that I started asking my mother who my father was. Since I was no longer living in my mother's home, where such things were not discussed, I finally developed the courage to talk to her about him. As a student of sociology I was studying the long-term impact of family relations. I did not want to go through life without knowing who my father was. I told my mother that I deserved to know.

"That's none of your business," my mother would say. She said it like she actually believed that my parentage had nothing to do with me and had no bearing on who I was.

How could it not have been my business? I wondered.

Years later, when I turned thirty-three and my mother was in her seventies and had since stopped drinking, she decided to tell me who my father was. I have written about this before, in *The World According to Me*, and I have come to see firsthand why my mother waited so long to tell me. My father was a famous musician during the 1960s. She met him on a one-night stand. He never knew me and I never met him.

When I first learned of my parentage, I was immediately bothered by what others would think; would they accuse me of making it up? Would my father's family think I wanted something from them?

All of those things happened. My mother finally did reveal to me that she did not tell me who my father was when I was younger because she wanted to save me from the rejection she had felt so many times. While she never contacted my father to tell him she was pregnant, she had experienced such denial from my brother Kevin's father and did not want to experience it again. She also did not want me to feel the rejection she felt as a child growing up without a father. I will not disclose my father's name here; it pulls attention away from the story to the salacious details of life.

My father was a great man. I have learned from others who knew him that he proudly represented the strength and dignity of blacks.

"Your daddy was a race man," one of his admirers once told me. "James Brown got the image of being black and proud when he sang [that song], but your daddy was the one who lived it."

I will never carry my father's last name, but spirit is much
more powerful than a name. The spirit and memories of our
ancestors run through the core of our being. Like it or not, our
parentage affects who we are and what we become. It is not imperative that we know them, but it is important if it is possible
to know who they are; that way we can learn from their
strengths and from their regrets. We can take the lessons of
their lives, and learn from their mistakes.

The history of black folks is all too disjointed, stopping
and starting over, rarely making direct links to the lessons of
the generation before. We must learn from the ancestors; we
must sit at their feet and listen to the accounts of their lives
and of the lives before them. Only then will we evolve as a
people.

My father's wife and family do not believe that I am his
child and I have no desire or need to prove it or to hurt them. I
believe what my mother said was true, that this great man is my
father, and for me that is enough. I've spent enough of my life
ignoring, denying, or regretting her truths. I've learned to let
life be.

We all need to know who we are and whose child we are.
The ancestors call out to us. When we can't or won't respond,
we are destined to repeat their mistakes. When we know them
and their stories, we can learn the lessons they teach without
suffering the same hardships.

I am convinced that we have in fact traded one slavery for
another. This is often by choice, but more often than not it is a

result of feeling like we have no choice. As a single parent to my adopted children, I understand what she meant.

When I agreed to take my sister's children in, I thought it would be a temporary situation lasting no more than two years. I made sure that the children had contact with their mother and tried to do the same with their fathers. Only two out of five of the fathers have made an effort to contact them. I reached out to the others but they did not respond. I have come to believe that family is as family does. My great-grandfather John Henry Freeman and the abolitionist John Hunn gave a hand to anyone in need. They saw family as all people who reached out in love.

Terry Evenson, the man who put me through college, became a grandfather to my children. He was a white man. My sisters Tanya and Christine have lived with or near me and helped to raise the children. They are mothers/aunts to my kids. My manager, Jeanine Chambers, is a sister to me and was a daughter to my mother, who helped to raise many children whom she did not give birth to. My mother dared anyone to say otherwise.

"That's my child," she said of Jeanine.

We'd often laugh about it because Jeanine, who has a light complexion and freckles, like my mother, looks more like her than I do.

It is important that we maintain our biological connections, but we, as human beings, share a bond of both blood and spirit. We must also surround ourselves with a family of kindheartedness. Just as John Hunn and others like him risked life and limb to keep families together, we must seek to connect to those who believe in liberation and life. Family must extend to those who give and those who need. When we do this, we give honor to the ancestors who fought, bled, and died for us to be free.

# FOURTEEN

# When History Repeats Itself

Your children are not your children.
They are the sons and daughters of Life's longing for itself.

—KHALIL GIBRAN, *THE PROPHET*

I never planned to be a mother. But all things are connected; they work together and in harmony. When I became a mother to my nieces and nephews and other children from similar backgrounds, I inherited the difficulties that come with alcohol and drug addiction. We have not paid enough attention to what has happened and what will happen to children who are held in utero under the influence of drugs. In our society, we treat one addiction or problem with another drug and expect the problem to go away when the symptoms diminish. Poverty and illiteracy are the new forms of slavery, and drug and alcohol addiction are its shackles. Drug addiction does not just affect the user; it has an impact on the entire family, crippling the children.

I've met many surrogate parents who struggle to enable their children to succeed. They struggle against learning disabilities and the costs involved with care. One of the unseen problems is the innate love that the foster or adopted child has for the biological parent. That unusually strong love exists to keep the parent connected for life. This love is a good and necessary thing; however, sometimes this bond leads the child to betray his own needs. The child's loyalty to the parent and her needs take precedence over anything else, even the child's success. Surrogate parents struggle in their role as secondary parent. When we work hard to maintain ties to the child's biological family, we run the risk of exposing him to heartaches that often come with those connections.

My children are still evolving into their own persons. They are finding their way in the world and growing into the people they want to be. As a sociologist, I had a hard time accepting that environment was not the main factor for how a child fares; biology plays a crucial role. Still, we must protect and guard our children at any cost. We cannot allow them to do or have whatever they think they want. Mine is the first generation of black parents to be afraid of our children. We complain about their lack of respect toward us, and then are shocked when they are disrespected by others.

During slavery, children were the responsibility of all the

adults. When a child's parents were sold away or died, other blacks on the plantation cared for them. This practice became a part of the black community until the seventies, when society became more "me"-centered. When we decided that the problems of others were not our own, we lost the sense of community that we brought from Africa, a sense of community that was maintained through the horrors of slavery.

We cannot solve every problem, but each of us must play our part in caring for our children. We must start now. Our future depends on it.

As a parent, I have learned much more and become a better parent than I would have imagined. My children have challenged me in many of the same ways that I challenged my mother. Once, I was stressed about getting my son into an exceptional private school, one that he desperately needed. After he was accepted, I was worried about being able to pay the expensive tuition. My mother was living with me and had long since turned her own life around. She had stopped drinking and had spent every day since becoming the person she was born to be. She took one look at me and began to chastise me.

"I know that look," she said. "That's the look of worry and stress. Worrying won't change a thing."

I told her she didn't understand; that my son's education was important to me. This son was already eight years old when he came to live with me and was seriously behind in his education. I explained to her that he needed this school to catch up. My mother shook her head and said that she may not have been able to put me in a fancy school, but she worried the same way about how we were going to eat and stay warm.

There are times when a painful memory can actually give you comfort; this was one of them. In that instance, I could see that in one generation, we had evolved many lifetimes. From my mother's time until mine, we had truly grown.

When my mother was living, I gave a party in her honor once a month. On her birthday, we'd throw a big bash complete with bands and entertainers. What my mother loved most about those parties was the gathering of like-minded people. She said she felt like she was a girl again, back in Delaware on her granddaddy's farm.

Once I asked my mother what she'd wanted to do and be when she was still a child. She smiled and sighed.

"I always wanted to have a big farm with lots of kids who needed a home," she said.

"Well," I said, laughing, "you got the lots of kids part right."

If we don't find our way in life, our dreams can turn against us. My mother had seven children and helped to raise others because she desired the love she felt with John Henry and Annie Mae. Like them, she turned no one away. We would be without electricity and heat, we'd have very little food, but if a friend of one of my siblings had no place to stay, my mother allowed her to live with us. "What's one more?" she'd ask.

It's this wonderful sentiment among the poor that often prohibits them from achieving what the rest of society would call success. I too have been blessed with the "Freeman" spirit.

If I'm not careful, though, that blessing can become a curse. It is important that we do all we can to help one another. But we can't do everything; we can't harbor the world. Often my feelings have ruled over my head and practical sense. My mother always took care of others, even when she was drinking. She did the best she could do, but she forgot to take care of herself.

I wonder where I would be if my ancestors didn't eat while feeding others. When we care for the community, we must also care for ourselves. I'm only now learning this lesson. I've come to see how critical it is to make certain that the giver also gets; otherwise life is out of balance.

The abolitionists John Hunn and Thomas Garrett were tried for assisting the Hawkins family, "fugitives" of slavery.

The trial was presided over by United States Supreme Court Justice Roger B. Taney, who later wrote the Dred Scott decision of 1856. Dred Scott was an enslaved black man who sued his owner, Dr. John Emerson, for his freedom. Emerson later turned the case over to his brother, John F. A. Sanford, hence the case name, *Dred Scott v. Sanford*. Taney and the Supreme Court ruled that people of African descent, whether they were slaves or not, could never be citizens of the United States and that Congress could have no authority to prohibit slavery in federal territories. The Dred Scott decision ruled that slaves were private property that could not be taken away from their owners without due process. It was also then ruled that slaves could not sue in court.

John Hunn and Thomas Garrett were up against a man who

was no friend to blacks, free or not. Hunn and Garrett were
found guilty under the Fugitive Slave Act of 1793, which held
the following:

> . . . *When a person held to labor in any of the United*
> *States . . . shall escape into any other said state or territory,*
> *the person to whom such labor or services may be due . . . is*
> *hereby empowered to seize or arrest such fugitive for labor . . .*
> *And be it further enacted, that any person who shall know-*
> *ingly and willfully obstruct such claimant . . . in seizing or ar-*
> *resting such fugitive from labor . . . shall forfeit and pay the*
> *sum of $500 [per offense].*

Hunn and Garrett were found guilty of both charges. Hunn
was found guilty of three lesser charges of feeding and shelter-
ing and Garrett was found guilty of seven counts of "stealing
property." Hunn's fines, however, caused him to lose his property. In a letter to William Still, John Hunn wrote,

> *I was twenty-seven years old when I engaged in the*
> *Underground Railroad business, and I have continued therein*
> *diligently until breaking up the business by the Great Rebellion.*
> *I then came to South Carolina to witness the uprising of a na-*
> *tion of slaves into the dignity and privileges of mankind.*
> *In this matter the course that I have pursued through life*
> *this far has given me solid satisfaction. I ask no other*
> *reward . . . than to feel that I have been of use to my fellow man.*

*No other course would have brought peace to my mind; then*
*why should any credit be awarded to me; or how can I count*
*any circumstances that may have occurred to me, in the light of*
*a sacrifice? If a man pursues the only course that will bring*
*peace to his own mind, is he deserving of any credit therefor? Is*
*not the reward worth striving for at any cost? Indeed it is, as I*
*well know . . .*

Hunn "vowed" never to withhold a helping hand from the
downtrodden in their hour of distress. He later moved to
South Carolina and became a successful farmer again. He
made the trip down to South Carolina to help newly freed
slaves find their place in America working for the Freedmen's
Bureau. In doing so, he was able to restore some of what he
lost. He moved back to Delaware near the end of his life. In
1901 through 1905, his son, also named John Hunn, became
the governor of the state of Delaware, whose legal system had
seen the Hunn family in ruin. He was responsible for signing
the Thirteenth, Fourteenth, and Fifteenth amendments into
the Delaware Constitution. Slavery had ended many years
before, but these amendments had not been signed into
Delaware's constitution until Governor Hunn did so. It must
be noted that the Fourteenth Amendment granted citizenship
and overturned the Dred Scott decision, the one written by the
same judge who ruled over John Hunn's case. Hunn was doing
the right thing at a time when many in society had said it was
wrong.

John Hunn stayed on the side of right.

I did not believe my mother's stories, but our beliefs can never change the facts; it is the facts that should change our beliefs.

Before I ever knew the whole story of John Hunn, I moved my family to Savannah and then to Richmond Hill, Georgia. We live about thirty miles from where John Hunn lived in South Carolina. I had been to St. Helena many times; I even spent a week on the beach with my mother near Hunn's home one month before she passed away. I was already writing this book, but did not know yet of Hunn's connections to the place so close to my new home.

When I first came to Savannah, I had suffered so much. My marriage was ending and my mother's health was slipping away. I had no idea that I was so close to the history of my past. Like John Hunn and my ancestors, I have often been compelled to do or say the right thing even when it was not popular; like them, I too am being restored. I am finding my way out of the bondage of the past.

# FIFTEEN

# Purpose Through Spirit

*Ain't got time to die, no I ain't got time to die . . .*
—NEGRO SPIRITUAL

We are all born with a purpose, a journey that must be completed. Once we learn the lessons of our journey, we are to pass them on to our children and the children around us. Too often, though, history has to start and stop, repeating itself until the lesson is learned. When we ignore the lessons of history, we are ignoring the things we need for ourselves today.

Even in my mother's drunkenness, she lived a righteous

life. My own "Pentecostal religiosity" did not allow me to see it. The do's and don'ts of my religious doctrine had blinded me to the pains of her heart. I was so spiritually-minded that I was no earthly good. I added educational degrees to my self-righteousness and ignored all the intelligence that had gone before me. To add insult to injury, I let black pride lord over the truth. But I have come back to my senses and can see the light. I can hear my mother's prayer:

"Divine Love always has and always will supply our every need. So let nothing hinder or delay the Divine Plan that the Creator has for your life today. We are moving on and on and on."

When my mother and I left the church we attended together in California, we began hosting a prayer group in our home along with my sister Jeanine. We didn't recognize it then, but our "prayer group" was very similar to a meeting of the Friends. We would gather every Saturday around six o'clock in the evening. We served plenty of food, and would discuss the joys and concerns in our lives. After we'd all share, my mother would pray her short prayer and all was well. Most gatherings went on until eleven p.m. and sometimes into the next morning.

When we first started meeting, we met with other Christians. Within a few weeks, people of other faiths and some agnostics asked if they could join us. We said of course and the small gathering kept growing. Our house became the place to be on a Saturday night. Attendees brought their children, who would gather in another room to discuss the problems they had and the ones they felt their parents put on them.

This was a special time. Folks went away "healed" of heartaches and troubles that plagued their minds and spirits. If someone came with a financial need, we discussed the best way to solve it.

"We don't need to pray 'bout this one," my mother would say. "We can fix this if we all work together."

We were a living example of the book of Acts and the lessons that Quaker founder George Fox tried to bring to the Church of England. We were also the African village and Native American tribe. Some nights we'd dance and sing, other times we'd cry with someone who'd unburdened the pain of abuse or loneliness. We were a community tied together in the belief that we needed one another. Without actually "knowing it," we all understood that the light we carried illuminated the way for those around us. At first, we thought there might be conversions to Christianity, and in a sense there were; we were living the teachings of Christ. But in a very true way, we accepted one another just as we were, not as anyone thought the other should be. The day we moved from San Diego, the prayer group all came to see us off. They lined our street crying as the moving trucks drove away.

Distance can never dampen Spirit; we are all still connected by Spirit and love.

What could this world be if we chose to live in harmony with our neighbors, concerned for the well-being of those who are in need? Slavery may have ended, but oppression has not. Racism, sexism, homophobia, poverty, and illiteracy still plague our nation and our hearts. In the spirit of the abolitionists, we must learn to be uncomfortable and embarrassed about the needs of others and be willing to help.

I am constantly asking myself how I can do more and do better. On a daily basis, I am letting go of my own "isms" and fears. I must be convicted by my own spiritual beliefs before ever teaching them and must never use them to judge or condemn. I must allow my education to be a light that guides but never blinds those who simply do not know. When faced with fear and opposition, I must stand for truth, no matter what the cost. Additionally, if I am to be forgiven, I must forgive. We must tell our own stories, while allowing others to tell theirs too, free from judgment or disbelief. When we learn to value our stories and our neighbors', then and only then will we be free.

So this is my story, my song of redemption . . . in it may you find your peace.

*My children, my children of Grace, you're gonna have to start the family over. It's on to you to set things straight.*

*Y'all done traded one slavery from another when you turned your back on wisdom. You ain't free to do what you want to do; you free to do what you supposed to do. Find out what you're here for, what you were sent for.*

*Take care of children. Just 'cause they don't come from you don't mean they don't belong to you. Come back to truth. Tell others that they can't hate their masters and want to be like him. Tell them all they did when they were slaves. How they worked together and take care of one another. Tell them all they do with nothing, and how they make everything work for somebody else. They can learn they history. Tell them to love, to forgive, to never forget.*

*They have to stand ground 'cause bigger change than they seen is coming. You the beginning of that change, but be careful. Change never comes without struggle . . . and joy never comes without pain.*

*In your lifetime you will see a big struggle, but you have each other to get through it.*

*Don't let the little things keep you from doing the big things. Others will try to stop you, but things are already moving; they can't be stopped. Everybody who looks like you is not on your side. And everybody who don't, ain't against you.*

*Talk to God and never stop loving. The more I write the more I see, the more I see the more I know everything is gonna be okay. I can feel it. I'm leaving these papers right here cause I know they gonna find you.*

*It's my time and I feel that, too. Learn from the past that's yours. Take the gift of what I done seen and use it to love. This is the Recipe of Life; the road to freedom. Freedom ain't just about living free it's about being free. The chains on our wrists ain't as strong as the chains on our mind. The only thing that can win over that evil is love. So learn to love, strive to love, 'cause we ain't got time for nothing else.* (From Redemption Song)

# NOTES TO THE READERS

I hope that by reading my story, and the story of my ancestors, you have been able to reflect on your own life and the lives of your family members. There is still much work to be done and many questions to be answered. I urge researchers of history to look closer at the individual stories written by the everyday people (both black and white) who lived during slavery. We must all take a closer look at the participation of our ancestors both for and against the abolition of the most "peculiar institution." The tendency in the past for blacks and whites in this country has been to look the other way where slavery is concerned. We can no longer afford to do so. Our lives, and the lives of our descendants, require us to learn from history so we do not repeat the mistakes of the past. Only then will we be able to evolve and become all that we were made for. Only then will we see that we are all connected in bondage and in freedom.

Further exploration in the area of slavery and abolition should conduct research that explores the following questions:

- *What percentage of whites were involved in abolishing slavery and to what degree?*
- *What percentage of unfree blacks made their way to freedom before emancipation? What percentage stayed on plantations when slavery ended, and why did they remain?*
- *How were enslaved blacks named? Did they choose their names or were they named after the slaveholders? (While popular "knowledge" argues that the majority of free blacks were named after the slaveholders, there is evidence that indicates that this was not the norm.)*

There are also personal questions that should be asked by the reader and his or her family:

- *Where is your family from?*
- *Where did they live during slavery? What were the laws of that state in regard to slavery?*

- *What role did your family play during the period of slavery and abolition?*
- *Where did you attend school? Who were your schools named after and what did those namesakes do or stand for?*
- *Where are your parents/grandparents from? What was their childhood like?*
- *What enslaves you? What have you enslaved yourself to?*
- *Whom do you need to forgive?*
- *What do you need to be forgiven for?*

The path to freedom has been paved by our ancestors. It requires forgiveness, understanding, wisdom, knowledge, faith, and most of all, love. In your search for answers may you find the peace you will need.

*I hope I have really been of some help to someone [more] than just family. God has been good to me. So I ask that you kids take time out to help someone. Pray for someone. Above all, love somebody. (From my mother's journal, May 9, 2002)*

# ACKNOWLEDGMENTS

This book has been a labor of love (emphasis on the word *labor*). I started it just after my second marriage and during my mother's illness, and I continued after her death. After all that, I also went through a divorce, and suffered a broken ankle, two moves, and a serious illness. There were many obstacles between me and the completion of this book. To get through the many "blocks," I went through counseling and therapy of all sorts, cranial/sacral massage, acupuncture, a psychologist, and meditation. In every session, by every practitioner, I was given similar information: You have a great task that you must complete and then you will be healed. One therapist (surprisingly, the psychologist) told me that the devil/enemy/ego was trying to keep me from my work.

This task has taken its toll, but it has also brought forth healing and recovery. Just as all things work together in life, they have also done so in this book.

I am indebted to the librarians and researchers who answered questions, found obscure references, and put up with what my old professor Dr. Mullins would call my "ignorance." I am especially grateful for those who were not aware that they had been conductors on my modern-day underground railroad with the information they provided. Women like Mary Ann Krah, whom I met at Red Mountain Spa when I gave a lecture there. After hearing me briefly mention the importance of the abolitionist movement, Mary Ann sent me her family's original 1835 copy of Elijah Porter Barrows's *A View of the American Slavery Question*. This little book helped shed a light on the perspective of many whites during that period.

I also "ran into" Phyllis Baker, Ph.D., at a restaurant one Saturday morning. I'd originally met Phyllis years before at the Miami Book Fair, where she'd introduced me to the audience. On that morning, Phyllis gave me a copy of her book *African American Spirituality, Thought and Culture*, which enabled me to understand my own religious/spiritual zeal and its connection to our past.

I am forever indebted to my "sister" and editor, Janet Hill Talbert, who patiently waited for this book long beyond its deadline and lovingly corralled me toward its completion. And to Christian Nwachukwu, who stepped in after Janet's retirement and brilliantly managed the book's completion. I am also grateful to my play "boyfriend" Bill and the folks at The Doubleday Publishing Group who believe in me and are continuously supportive of black history and literature. (Big Ups! We can't do it by ourselves.)

I am fortunate to have found my sister Jeanine Chambers, and fortunate for her gifts. Without her typing and editing, you'd be reading my really bad longhand. Without her prayers, laughter (snorting), ice cream runs, and love, my work would be incomplete.

I am grateful for all of my children, but on this one Fatima and Jabril, who had to lower their voices, find their own food, and keep me in tea and popcorn until I was done.

Thanks also to my agent, Victoria Sanders, who I'm certain is a descendant of John Hunn.

To my sisters Christine Berry, Tanya Berry, and Rocki Rockingham, thank you for your support and love throughout this journey called life.

And to all of our ancestors, both black and white, who risked life and limb for our liberation.

To my incredible mother, Beatrice Berry, and abolitionist John Hunn, may I live to make you proud.

And to Mariah, who left too soon.

NOTES

The following notes are references to the sources of each chapter. I have also included some background information, which if included in the body of the book may have led the reader away from the major points expressed. The references and background notes do not detail every aspect of the story or the research for it. I have sought to include those aspects that may be of further interest to the reader.

## Preface

Terry Evenson, the wealthy benefactor who helped put me through college, is mentioned in later chapters. Terry also funded the education of other African Americans, Native Americans, Latinos, and immigrant children. He took a one-on-one approach to his scholarship program. Terry died in 2004 and is dearly missed. His partner, Jim Keinz, is still close to me and my family, as are his children, Vida and Allen. His ex-wife, Penny Evenson, is an incredible singer in Greece and is also a part of our very eclectic family. Terry's support enabled me to get an education. His love and direction guided me toward a love of art, nature, and bird-watching.

## Introduction

In pinpointing the timeline for the freedom of African Americans several sources were used, including the *Negro Heritage Library*, vol. 1.

There is an excellent timeline on *Slavery and the Making of America* at www.pbs.org./wnet/slavery/timeline.

For a wonderful look at African American lives from 1900 to the present, look at *The African American Century* by Henry Louis Gates Jr. and Cornel West. The book *Freedom Days* by Janus Adams, in which she outlines 365 inspired moments in Civil Rights history, is also a great resource.

The Truth and Reconciliation Commission is no longer

active, but a full report of the commission is posted at
www.info.gov.za/otherdocs/2003/trc. In the forward, written
by Bishop Desmond Tutu, he writes, "For the sake of our
[South Africans'] stability, it is fortunate that the kinds of details exposed by the Commission did not come out in a series
of criminal trials which . . . most likely would have ended in
acquittals." He continues, "It is something of a pity that . . .
the white community failed to take advantage of the Truth and
Reconciliation process . . . many of them carry a burden of
guilt which would have been assuaged had they actively em-
braced the opportunities offered . . . those who do not con-
sciously acknowledge any sense of guilt are in a sense worse off
than those who do."

When you read this report, and you must, you will begin to
comprehend not only what South Africans endured under
apartheid, but you will also see the importance of a system that
works through truth and reconciliation rather than guilt and
revenge.

*Chapter One: The Gift*

The opening quote, from Manetta Gannaway Pollard, is an
alias for my editor Janet Hill Talbert (who felt odd being
quoted in the book). Janet recently retired from Doubleday after twenty-two years. All of my Doubleday books were edited
by her. She is an incredible conductor on the modern-day underground railroad. A great deal of important information

and wonderful literature has found its way onto our shelves through the hands of Janet Hill Talbert. She is a book warrior; I'm so glad she's on the side of right.

Much of the information here comes from my life and conversations with my mother. She was treated at Memorial Hospital and St. Joseph's/Candler in Savannah, Georgia. The staff in those hospitals, and hospitals throughout America, are to be commended for the compassionate care they give to those who are sick and/or dying. Many stood around with Bernita, Jeanine, and me singing, laughing, and sharing in my mother's last hour.

There is a tremendous problem with the health care in this country; unfortunately the hospital staff and caregivers often bear the burden of problems they did not cause. Poverty, unemployment, problems associated with being uninsured and underinsured, and poor health-care habits (40 percent of chronic illnesses are behavior-related) all end up on the steps of American hospitals. Many inner-city and rural hospitals are in danger of being shut down. We must find a way to deal with the complex crisis associated with health care, and when we do, we must show appreciation to the men and women who tirelessly care for our health.

The passage I read to my mother is from a letter Mary Baker Eddy wrote to follower Adam H. Dickey. It can be found on the Christian Science Healing Unlimited Web page at www.christianscience.org/MBE2AHD.htm.

*Chapter Two: Pain Before Beauty*

The PBS documentary I saw was *Slavery and the Making of America,* directed by William H. Grant.

*Chapter Three: Burdens Down, Lord, Burdens Down*

My brother Kevin no longer cries when asked to sing. He recently retired after thirty years of service in the United States Marine Corps. OOH-RAH!

The discussion about spirituality and African Americans comes from *African-American Spirituality, Thought & Culture* by sociologist Phyllis Baker. In the book, Baker looks at African American spirituality through the eyes of an African American who is also spiritual. Like Zora Neale Hurston before her, she allows her experience to guide her to the research and then becomes objective enough to speak truth to power. The book includes rituals and prayer for moving from bondage to liberation. Also look at the works of psychologist Na'im Akbar, especially *Breaking the Chains of Psychological Slavery*.

Information on Peter Spencer and the African United Methodist Protestant Church comes from the church's library in Wilmington, Delaware.

The information about the Church of God in Christ comes from documents from the Mother Church of God in Christ in Wilmington, Delaware, and the official Web site for the church: www.cogic.org.

Information on Crozer Theological Seminary can be found at www.oldchesterpa.com/schools_crozer_seminary.htm.

For an amazing paper written by Dr. Martin Luther King Jr. on the influence of Greek mythology in Christian thought while at Crozer, see *The Papers of Martin Luther King, Jr.: Volume One: Called to Serve*, edited by Claybourne Carson, Ralph Luker, and Penny A. Russell.

The quote from Paulo Coelho comes from his book *The Alchemist*, a wonderful tale of purpose and destiny.

The research study I worked on with Dr. Mullins was in *Phylon*, vol. 46, no. 3, and is titled *The American Black Elite, 1930–1978*. Dr. Mullins also served as chair of the committee for my dissertation but passed away shortly before I defended. (Paul Sites, her coauthor, took her place.) Both were certainly conductors on my railroad to freedom.

Information regarding the abolition of slavery by state can be found in the *Negro Heritage Library*, vol. 1, and in *Slavery and Freedom in Delaware, 1639–1865*, by William H. Williams. Also see *Letters from the Slave States* by James Stirling, written in 1857, in which he chronicles his travels throughout the South. His eyewitness account of slavery is insightful, honest, and at times uplifting.

When commenting on the generation gap Stirling notes, "The young of the South is opposed to the old. . . . Among the aristocracy of the South, pride of intellect and pride of station may help to perpetuate hereditary error; but the young farmers of the hills and the young farmers of the towns, have opened their eyes to the curse that is

upon them, and assuredly, they will not rest until it is an-
nulled."

Another excellent source for an eyewitness account of slav-
ery is *Remembering Slavery: African Americans Talk About Their
Personal Experiences of Slavery and Emancipation*, edited by Ira
Berlin, Marc Favreau, and Steven Miller.

*Chapter Four: Songs of Freedom*

Information and lyrics from encoded slave songs came from the
site www.negrospirituals.com and Barbara Bacon's discussion
of slave code songs for young readers at www.voicesacrosstime
.org. I also utilized the work of *Slave Songs of the United States* by
Allen, et al., originally published in 1867. I love music and am
especially fond of the spirituals. There are many wonderful
spirituals that are rarely sung and hardly remembered. Many of
these songs were taught to me by my mother; I miss singing
them with her.

Much of the discussion on the Underground Railroad came
from William Still's book, *The Underground Railroad*, originally
published in 1872, then again in 1968, and most recently in
2007.

I am happy to see that the book is also available for
Amazon's Kindle. Still's book is essential to understanding the
workings of those individuals who toiled for freedom. It includes firsthand accounts of fugitives from slavery document-
ing their travels and the names of the loved ones they left
behind.

*The Underground Railroad* also names those barely known conductors and stationmasters of freedom. Additionally, it lists the names of slaveholders and describes in detail their treatment toward the enslaved blacks. Every American household should own a copy of this book.

There is also a William Still Foundation and National Underground Railroad Family Reunion Festival; for more information go to www.undergroundrr.com.

Information on the workings of the Underground Railroad also came from the book *Station Master on the Underground Railroad: The Life and Letters of Thomas Garrett* by James A. McGowan and from *The Underground Railroad in Delaware, Maryland and West Virginia* by William J. Suitala. Additional sources include *History of the Underground Railroad in Chester and the Neighboring Counties of Pennsylvania* by Robert Smedley and *The Underground Railroad from Slavery to Freedom* by Wilbur H. Siebert.

The recorded confession of Nat Turner can be found at www.melanet.com/nat.html.

For an in-depth and enlightening look at William Styron's Pulitzer Prize–winning novel about Nat Turner, please read William Styron's *Nat Turner: Ten Black Writers Respond*. It includes essays from the great minds of John Henry Clarke, Lerone Bennett Jr., Alvin Poussaint, Vincent Harding, John Olive Killens, John A Williams, Ernest Kaiser, Loyle Hairshon, Charles V. Hamilton, and Mike Thewell.

*Chapter Five: My Native Land*

The initial information on John Hunn came from the Wilmington Public Library, University of Delaware Archives, and www.wikipedia.org.

Historical information on the state of Delaware comes from *Slavery and Freedom in Delaware, 1639–1865*, by William Williams, and Marion Bjornson's 1928 master's thesis at the University of Delaware, "The Underground Railroad in Delaware." Also see *A House Divided: Slavery and Emancipation in Delaware, 1638–1865*, by Patience Essah.

For an illuminating presentation on the horrible voyage of enslaved Africans to America, see Marcus Rediker's *The Slave Ship: A Human History*, in which he concludes, "Reparations are, in my view, in order, but justice cannot be reduced to a calculus of money, lest proposed solutions play by the rules of the game that spawned the slave trade in the first place."

*Chapter Six: Setting the Captives Free*

Information on the life of John Huston came from "Quakers in Delaware, 1672–1872," by Alice Jaquette Lindole, and Ezra Michener's *A Retrospect of Early Quakerism*. The article "Quakers in Delaware in the time of William Penn" by Herbert C. Standing in *Delaware History*, vol. 20, no.2, is also a source of information.

For an in-depth look at the history, beliefs, and customs of the Religious Society of Friends, go to their Web site, www.quaker.org, and find out more about the religious witnesses for peace since 1660.

## Chapter Seven: Set the Captives Free

The main sources for information on the Quakers and the Pennsylvania Vigilance Committee were those listed for chapter six.

## Chapter Eight: Free Your Mind

My sister Myrna passed away in 1992. She is in that cloud of witnesses with my mother and our ancestors. When I sit down to write, I sit under one of Myrna's paintings. It is a black Madonna and child. When I was about four or five years old, I posed for the features of the baby.

Myrna was a brilliant artist and photographer, and an incredible being. She often referred to me as the child she wished she'd had. She died from complications with diabetes and alcoholism. She sought beauty, truth, and freedom but suffered a great deal of pain. Myrna is now free, and her memory lives on.

Information on my schools in Delaware came from archives in the Wilmington Public Library, but you can also go to www.oldwilmington.net.

Chapter Nine: Go Back to Move Forward

The primary sources for this chapter were conversations with my mother and her journals. My mother's journals were a wonderful find. From time to time, I flip to a page to "find" the wisdom I need.

Today I came up with this passage: "I have so many more hills to climb, but with love I will make it. Anyone who just sits around all day and thinks about their self needs to focus on other things . . . Pray instead; your days will be so much better."

Every time I read her journals, I uncover something new. In the corners, folds, and pockets of each book I find notes, receipts, and sometimes pictures.

When I first found her journals, I decided to save these bits for later times.

Today, I found a picture of Myrna—my ancestors are truly with me.

Census information can be found at your local library and at www.ancestry.com. To find facts and figures about the United States Census Bureau, go to their Web site, www.census.gov.

Also see Tony Burroughs's *Black Roots: A Beginner's Guide to Tracing the African American Family Tree*, 2001.

*Chapter Ten: The Aftermath; and Chapter Eleven:
Sometimes I Feel Like a Motherless Child*

The primary sources of these chapters were conversations
with my mother and her journals. I cannot stress enough the
importance of talking to your older relatives. They carry the
stories and wisdom we need. Ask questions and take the time
to listen. If you don't know what to ask, get a copy of *201
Questions to Ask Your Kids/201 Questions to Ask Your Parents* by
Pepper Schwartz.

*Chapter Twelve: Family Ties*

The sources of the narratives of enslaved blacks are listed in
the chapter. For other firsthand accounts, see *Drums and
Shadows: Survival Stories Among the Georgia Coastal Negroes*,
from the Georgia Writers' Project (many of these stories have
been criticized for their methodology; still, they should be
read for what folks had to say about their own lives). Also make
sure you own a copy of *Great Slave Narratives*, edited by Arna
Bontemps. (Americans don't understand the impact of slavery
because we often refuse to learn about slavery. It's imperative
that we all know this history; it is not black history, it's
American history.)

*Chapter Thirteen: Family Matters, Color Counts*

Most of the stories referenced in this chapter came from *The Underground Railroad* by William Still.

For information on Benjamin Banneker, please read Silvio A. Bedini's book, *The Life of Benjamin Banneker: The First African-American Man of Science*.

*Chapter Fourteen: When History Repeats Itself*

Sources here are Still's *The Underground Railroad* and *The American Slave Code in Theory and Practice* by William Goodell.

*Chapter Fifteen: Purpose Through Spirit*

The group in San Diego broke up after I, and then later Jeanine, moved to Savannah, Georgia. We continued the work when we opened Iona's Gallery, a fine-art and great-finds gallery we ran until our mom passed away. Jeanine and I used the proceeds from the gallery to help homeless families get back on their feet. We also used the space for lectures, jam sessions, and gatherings similar to the ones we held in San Diego. We closed the physical space, but have continued to represent artists with shows at each of our homes. We have continued to host spiritual gatherings and help others in need.

# BIBLIOGRAPHY

Abel, Robert H. *Freedom Dues or A Gentleman's Progress in the New World*. New York: The Dial Press, 1984.

Adams, Janus. *Freedom Days: 365 Inspired Moments in Civil Rights History*. New York: John Wiley & Sons, Inc., 1998.

Adams, Virginia M., ed. *On the Altar of Freedom: A Black Soldier's Civil War Letters from the Front: Corporal James Henry Gooding*. New York: Warner Books, 1991.

Akbar, Na'im. *Breaking the Chains of Psychological Slavery*. Tallahassee, FL: Mind Productions & Associates, Inc., 1999.

Allan, William Frances (compiler), Charles Pickard Ware (compiler), and Lucy McKim Garrison (compiler). *Slave Songs of the United States*. Carlisle, MA: Applewood Books, 1996.

Altman, Susan. *The Encyclopedia of African-American Heritage*. Facts on File, 1997.

Arott, Kathleen. *African Myths and Legends*. Oxford University Press, 1990.

Austin, Lettie. *The Black Man and the Promise of America*. Glenview, IL: Scott Foresman and Company, 1970.

Barrows, Elijah Porter. *A View of the American Slavery Question*. New York: John S. Taylor, 1836.

Bedini, Silvio A. *The Life of Benjamin Banneker: The First African-American Man of Science*. Maryland Historical Society, 2005.

Berlin, Ira, Marc Favreau, and Steven Miller. *Remembering Slavery*. New York: The New Press, 1998.

Bjornson, Marion L. "The Underground Railroad in Delaware." Master's thesis, University of Delaware, 1928.

Blight, William. *Race and Reunion: The Civil War in American Memory*. Cambridge: The Belknap Press of Harvard University, 1999.

Bontemps, Arna. *Great Slave Narratives*. Boston: Beacon Press, 1969.

Branch, Taylor. *Parting the Waters: America in the King Years, 1954–1963*. New York: Simon and Schuster, 1988.

Brown, William Wells. *Clotel: Or, The President's Daughter: A Narrative of Slave Life in the United States*. New York: University Books Title, 1995.

Burroughs, Tony. *Black Roots: A Beginner's Guide to Tracing the African American Family Tree*. New York: Simon and Schuster, 2001.

Clinton, Catherine. *Harriet Tubman: The Road to Freedom*. New York: Back Bay Books, 2005.

Coelho, Paulo. *The Alchemist*. San Francisco: HarperCollins, 1988.

Conrad, Earl. *Harriet Tubman: Negro Soldier and Abolitionist*. New York: International Publishers, 1976.

Cosby, Bill, and Alvin F. Poissant, M.D. *Come On People: On the Path from Victims to Victors*. Nashville: Tomas Nelson, 2007.

Davis, John P., ed. *Negro Heritage Library: The American Negro Reference Book,* vols. I and II. Englewood Cliffs, NJ: Prentice-Hall, 1966.

Delaware State Museums. "Sources Relating to Interpretation of the

Trials of John Hunn and Thomas Garrett at the New Castle County Court House," compiled 1985.

Dyson, Michael Eric. *I May Not Get There with You: The True Martin Luther King Jr.* New York: The Free Press, 2000.

Ely, Melvin Patrick. *Israel on The Appomattox: A Southern Experiment in Black Freedom from the 1790s through the Civil War.* New York: Alfred A. Knopf, 2004.

Essah, Patience. *A House Divided: Slavery and Emancipation in Delaware, 1638–1865.* Charlottesville, VA: University Press of Virginia, 1966.

Fauchauld, Nick. *William Lloyd Garrison: Abolitionist and Journalist.* Minneapolis: Compass Point Books, 2005.

Foner, Eric. *Reconstruction: America's Unfinished Revolution: 1863–1877.* New York: Harper and Row, 1988.

Ford, Clyde W. *The Hero with an African Face: Mythic Wisdom of Traditional Africa.* New York: Bantam Books, 1999.

Frazier, E. Franklin. *Black Bourgeoisie.* New Frazier, E. Franklin. *The Negro Family in the United States* (revised and abridged ed.). Chicago: University of Chicago Press, 1967.

Gates Jr., Henry Louis, and Cornel West. *The African American Century: How Black Americans Have Shaped Our Country.* New York: The Free Press, 2000.

Genovese, Eugene D. *The World the Slaveholders Made: Two Essays in Interpretation.* Middletown, CT: Wesleyan University Press, 1988.

Georgia Writers' Project. *Drums and Shadows: Survival Studies Among the Georgia Coastal Negroes.* Athens, GA: Brown Thrasher Books, University of Georgia, 1986.

Giddings, Paula. *When and Where I Enter . . . The Impact of Black Women on Race and Sex in America.* New York: William Morris and Company, Inc., 1984.

Goldberg, Mel. *John Brown's Raid.* Garden City, NY: Nelson Doubleday Inc., 1961.

Goldwin, Robert A., ed. *100 Years of Emancipation.* Chicago: Rand McNally, 1963.

Goodall, William. *Michigan Historical Reprint Series: The American*

*Slave Code in Theory and Practice: Its distinctive features shown by its statutes, judicial decisions, and illustrative facts.* Scholarly Publishing Office, University of Michigan Library, March 2006.

Gwaltney, John Langston. *Drylongso: A Self-Portrait of Black America.* New York: Vintage Books, 1980.

Hampton, Henry, and Steve Fayer. *Voices of Freedom: An Oral History of the Civil Rights Movement from the 1950's through the 1980's.* New York: Bantam Books, 1990.

Helper, Hinton Rowan. *The Impending Crisis of the South: How to Meet It.* New York: A.B. Burdick, 1860.

Hord, Fred Lee (Mzeehasana Okpara), and Jonathan Scott Lee, eds. *I Am Because We Are: Readings in Black Philosophy.* Amherst, MA: University of Massachusetts Press, 1995.

Hurmence, Belinda. *My Folks Don't Want Me to Talk About Slavery: Twenty-one Oral Histories of Former North Carolina Slaves.* Winston-Salem, NC: John F. Blair, 2002.

Johnson, Michael P., and James L. Roard. *Black Masters: A Free Family of Color in the Old South.* New York: W.W. Norton and Company, 1984.

Johnson, Walker, ed. *The Chattel Principle: Internal Slave Trades in the Americas.* New Haven: Yale University Press, 2004.

Keckley, Elizabeth. *Behind the Scenes, Or, Thirty Years a Slave, and Four Years in the White House.* New York: Penguin Books, 2005.

Kemble, Frances Anne. *Journal of Residence on a Georgian Plantation in 1833–1839.* Edited by John A. Scott. Athens, GA: University of Georgia Press, 1984.

Lacy, Dan. *The White Use of Blacks in America: 350 Years of Law and Violence, Attitudes and Etiquette, Policies and Change.* New York: Atheneum, 1992.

Larson, Kate Clifford. *Bound for the Promised Land: Harriet Tubman, Portrait of an American Hero.* New York: Ballantine Books, 2004.

Lenski, E. Gerhard. *Power and Privilege: A Theory of Social Stratification.* New York: Bantam Books, 1990.

Levine, Lawrence. *The Black Culture and Black Consciousness: Afro-*

*American Folk Thought from Slavery to Freedom.* Oxford: Oxford University Press, 1977.

Levy, Andrew. *The First Emancipator: The Forgotten Story of Robert Carter: The Founding Father Who Freed His Slaves.* New York: Random House, 2005.

Lindell, Alice Jaquette. "Quakers in Delaware, 1672–1872." Master's thesis, University of Delaware, 1957.

Long, Richard A., ed. *Black Writers and the American Civil War.* Secaucus, NJ: Blue and Grey Press, 1988.

Loury, Beverly. *Harriett Tubman: Imagining a Life.* New York: Doubleday, 2007.

McGill, Alice, and Michael Cummings (ill). *In The Hollow of Your Hand: Slave Lullabies.* Boston: Houghton Mifflin Co., 2000.

McGowan, James A. *Station Masters on the Underground Railroad: The Life and Letters of Thomas Garrett.* Jefferson, NC: McFarland & Company, Inc., 2005.

Michener, Ezra. *A Retrospect of Early Quakerism.* Philadelphia: T. Ellwood Zell, 1860.

Mullane, Deirdre. *Crossing the Danger Water: Three Hundred Years of African American Writing.* New York: Doubleday/Anchor Books, 1993.

Owens, William A. *Black Mutiny: The Revolt on the Schooner Amistad.* New York: Plume, 1968.

Patterson, Orlando. *Rituals of Blood: Consequences of Slavery in Two American Centuries.* Washington, DC: Civitas Counterpoint, 1998.

Pickney, Andrew, and Stephen Alcorn (ill). *Let It Shine: Stories of Black Women Freedom Fighters.* San Diego: Gulliver Books, 2000.

Pollitzer, William. *The Gullah People and Their African Heritage.* Athens, GA: University of Georgia Press, 1999.

Pope-Hennessy, James. *Sins of the Fathers: A Study of the Atlantic Slave Traders, 1441–1807.* New York: Barnes & Noble Books, 1998.

Rediker, Marcus. *The Slave Ship.* New York: Viking /Penguin Group, 2007.

Schafer, Judith Kelleher. *Becoming Free, Remaining Free: Manumission and Enslavement in New Orleans, 1846–1862.* Baton Rouge, LA: Louisiana State University Press, 2003.

Schwartz, Pepper. *201 Questions to Ask Your Kids/201 Questions to Ask Your Parents*. New York: Avon Books, 2001.

Siebert, Wilbur H. *The Underground from Slavery to Freedom*. New York: Arno Press, and *The New York Times*, 1963 reprint.

Sites, Paul, and Elizabeth I. Mullins. *The Black American Elite, 1930–1978* (Phylon), vol. 46, no. 3 (3rd quarter, 1985). Atlanta: Clark Atlanta University.

Slaughter, Thomas P. *Bloody Dawn: The Christiana Riot and Racial Violence in the Antebellum North*. Oxford: Oxford University Press, 1991.

Smedley, Robert C. *History of the Underground Railroad in Chester and the Neighboring Counties of Pennsylvania*. Lancaster, PA: Office of the Journal, 1883.

Standing, Herbert C. *Quakers in Delaware in the Time of William Penn*, Delaware History, vol. 20., no. 2 (1982).

Still, William. *The Underground Railroad: A Record of Facts, Authentic Narratives, Letters, & C.* Philadelphia: Porter and Coates, 1872.

Stirling, James. *Letters from the Slave States*. London: Savill and Edwards Printing, 1857.

Switala, William. *Underground Railroad in Delaware, Maryland and West Virginia*. Mechanicsburg, PA: Stackpole Books, 2004.

Theisman, Howard. *Meditations of the Heart*. Boston: Beacon Press, 1953.

Thomas, Hugh. *The Slave Trade: The Story of the Atlantic Slave Trade: 1440–1870*. New York: Touchstone, 1997.

Tobin, Jacqueline L., and Raymond G. Dobard. *Hidden in Plain View: A Secret Story of Quilts and the Underground Railroad*. New York: Doubleday, 1999.

Wade-Gayles, Gloria. *My Soul is a Witness: African American Women's Spirituality*. Boston: Beacon Press, 1995.

Wagstaff, Thomas. *Black Power: The Radical Response to White America*. Beverly Hills: Glencoe Press, 1969.

Walker, Alice. *In Search of Our Mothers' Gardens: Womanist Prose*. Orlando, FL: Harcourt Brace Jovanovich, 1983.

Williams, William H. *Slavery and Freedom in Delaware: 1639–1865*. Wilmington, DE: Scholarly Resources, Inc., 2001.

Wilson, Amos N. *Blueprint for Black Power: A Moral, Political and Economic Imperative for the Twenty-first Century*. New York: Afrikan World Infosystems, 1998.

Winch, Julie. *A Gentleman of Color: The Life of James Forten*. Oxford: Oxford University Press, 2002.

Woodson, Carter. *The Mis-Education of the Negro*. Trenton, NJ: Agwan World Press, Inc., 1933.

# ABOUT THE AUTHOR

BERTICE BERRY, PH.D., is an inspirational speaker, sociologist, and former stand-up comedienne. She is also the author of four works of nonfiction and four novels: *Redemption Song*, *The Haunting of Hip Hop*, *Jim and Louella's Homemade Heart-Fix Remedy*, and, most recently, *When Love Calls, You Better Answer*. She lives in Richmond Hill, Georgia.